DANCE OF THE TRUSTEES

FRONTISPIECE. Miami Township map.

Dance of the Trustees

*On the Astonishing Concerns
of a Small Ohio Township*

Dylan Taylor-Lehman

TRILLIUM, AN IMPRINT OF
THE OHIO STATE UNIVERSITY PRESS
COLUMBUS

Copyright © 2018 by The Ohio State University.
All rights reserved.
Trillium, an imprint of The Ohio State University Press.

Library of Congress Cataloging-in-Publication Data is available online at
catalog.loc.gov.

Cover design by Laurence J. Nozik
Text design by Juliet Williams
Type set in Adobe Sabon and ITC Clearface

In a word, no spot in Ohio has more beauty and attractiveness for the sightseer, or charm for the piscatorial sportsman or sentimental lover, or information for the geologist, botanist, or philosopher.

—"Miami Township" section of *Greene County 1803–1908*

No more interesting or instructive matter could be presented to an intelligent public. In this volume will be found a record of many whose lives are worth the imitation of coming generations. . . . It tells of those in every walk of life who have striven to succeed, and records how that success has usually crowned their efforts. . . .

Coming generations will appreciate this volume and preserve it as a sacred treasure, from the fact that it contains so much that would never find its way into public records, and which would otherwise be inaccessible.

—Preface to *Portrait and Biographical Album of Greene and Clark Counties, Ohio*

Except for those individuals who like to hear the sound of their own voice, most of us want to deal with the items on the agenda, solve the problems if we can, and go about our business.

—"FAQ: How to Run a Meeting" section of the *Ohio Township Trustee Sourcebook*

Public

1. Call to Order

2. Adoption of the Minutes – August 17th, 2015

3. Motion to Approve Payment of Bills - $68,854.94
        1000 - General - $7,619.42
        2191 - Fire - $32,891.77
        2042 – Cemetery - $7,694.25
        2281 – EMS Billing – $7,688.89
        Road and Bridge – $12,960.61
            2011 – Motor Vehicle License - $27.39
            2021 - Gas Tax – $1,935.46
            2031- Road and Bridge – $10,997.76
            2231 – Permissive - $0

4. Correspondence
    The Trustees received:
- Ohio Township News magazine;
- "Grassroots Clippings"— OTA's monthly newsletter;
- Bricker & Eckler newsletter;
- Ohio LTAP Newsletter;
- Greene Burial Council newsletter;
- League of Women Voters newsletter;
- Michigan State University survey;
- Anthem newsletter re: Ohio HMO Exchange Networks;
- E-Mail from Unum acknowledging cancellation of policy;
- E-Mail from OneAmerica acknowledging approval of life insurance policy;
- E-Mails from MVRPC re: September Board meeting agenda; news release re: Bronze Level award; news release re: Public Participation meeting announcement; news release re: Dayton Area Board of Realtors' membership with MVRPC;
- GC Association Township Dinner announcement;
- E-Mail from GC Association re: 09/04/15 Legislative Alert and Info
- County Auditor's 2016 Budget Hearings schedule;
- E-Mail from County Auditor's office re: 2016 Local Government Alternative Allocation;
- E-Mail from RPCC re: move of Executive Committee to September 9th;
- RPCC meeting announcement;
- Proposed amendments to RPCC Bylaws;

FIGURE 1. Meeting agenda (front).

- Greene County Combined Health District's meeting announcement and Commissioner's monthly newsletter;
- E-Mail to GPRS requesting survey work at Glen Forest Cemetery;
- E-Mail to and from Mitch Cosler re: survey work and invoice;
- E-Mail to and from Lisa Goldberg re: Bike Route Designation Meeting;
- July 21st Zoning Commission meeting minutes;
- E-Mail from Ann Lisa Piercy re: Township Trustees' and Zoning Commission meeting minutes;
- E-Mail confirming registration for the Ohio Chapter 2015 Snow and Ice Conference; *9/29/15*
- Fund Status, Revenue Status and Appropriation Status reports for September 9th, 2015.

5. Fire Department Report

58 EMT incidents since last meeting
24 Fire

6. Cemetery-Road Report

5 burials since last meeting =
"2 ashes, 2 burials, Ashes in Clifton"

Company came in and found 35 unmarked graves; 25 in areas marked for sale. Obviously we've marked where we found these people. Only looked where asked them to live.

7. Fiscal Officer's Report *"no progress on the disinterment"*

Resolution 2015-14: Amendment of Permanent Appropriations. *increase in various funds across many departments*
~~Resolution 2015-15: Transfer of Funds.~~ *transfer 10K from Gen. Fund to Glen Forest Cemetery*

8. Zoning Inspector's Report (First meeting of each month)

Ongoing Violations of the Miami Township Zoning Resolution at 1221 Glen Road. *1 permit issued since last meeting*

9. Standing Committee Reports (Second Meeting of each month)
  * MVRPC – TAC Committee
  * MVRPC – Executive Committee
  * MVRPC – Board of Director's
  * Greene County Regional Planning & Coordinating Commission
  * YS Senior Center
  * Clifton-Union Cemetery
  * YS-Miami Township Community Resources
  * Grinnell Mill

10. New Business

11. Old Business

12. Adjournment........next meeting scheduled for September 21st, 2015.

FIGURE 2. Meeting agenda (back).

CONTENTS

ACKNOWLEDGMENTS

A seriously limitless thank-you to the librarians, historians, editors, and writers for assisting me in this hard-to-explain endeavor. You not only helped me with this project but greatly improved my own life by giving me so much to wonder about. I truly appreciate the role you played in putting this project together. Special thanks to Chris Mucher for reading the manuscript and making a list of exactly fifty-nine corrections/changes needed to make the book as accurate as possible.

To Diane, Lauren, and Audrey—everything I write reflects your guidance. Thanks for your friendship and thanks for giving me a chance.

The following is a true and accurate account of the *Proceedings of the Miami Township Board of Trustees Meeting* that took place on Wednesday, September 9, 2015. The book follows the format of the agenda for that specific meeting. Nothing has been embellished or altered for narrative purposes.

An Unusual Crowd

The Miami Township Trustee meeting of September 9, 2015, took place in a squat, cinderblock room attached to the Miami Township Fire and Rescue firehouse. The meeting room had parquet floors and a drop ceiling and was decorated with serviceably framed firefighter ephemera. A small corridor on the east side of the room led to the trustees' offices, and it was in this doorway that Chris Mucher and Mark Crockett, two of the three Miami Township trustees, were milling around, chatting until it was time to take their seats at a table at the head of the room. The township's third trustee, Lamar Spracklen, was sitting the meeting out for personal reasons. Crockett looked out at the room and slowly scratched his chin.

A township is a municipal subdivision, jointly overseen by trustees who meet twice a month to keep the township running. Miami Township is a township of twenty-four square miles in northern Greene County, a county in southwestern Ohio not far from Dayton. Miami Township trustees oversee every aspect of the township's needs, from maintaining its cemeteries to winterizing its roads. They oversee the fire department, run an inn, and balance the needs of farmers and developers. Historically, each meeting's agenda reflects the scope of the trustees' concerns, and the agenda of Wednesday, September 9, 2015, as discussed in this book, ran a page and a half, with twelve enumerated sections. It

FIGURE 3. Entrance to the offices of the Miami Township Board of Trustees. Photo by Dylan Taylor-Lehman.

was a lot of ground to cover, but the trustees had over thirty years of experience between them and could ordinarily get through the meeting in under an hour. It wasn't that they cut corners but that they could trust each other to get township business done, whatever it was, without surfeit discussion.

Except, on that particular September evening, it wasn't business as usual. By 6:45 p.m., fifteen minutes before the meeting was scheduled to start, a small crowd had assembled outside the building. People talked in clusters, and a new person walked down the sidewalk every few minutes to join them. The air was charged with excitement, the buzz of people gathering for a common cause. A years-long controversy had come to a head, and people were there to take sides.

Each person who arrived was visibly surprised by the crowd already gathered. In fact, it was strange that there was anyone there at all. Mucher, then in his nineteenth year as a trustee, said it was the first meeting of 2015 that had drawn anyone from the public. Not one person had attended a meeting who hadn't been officially obligated to be there. The *Yellow Springs News*, the local paper of record whose office is a few hundred feet up the street, used to cover the meetings but stopped because, as one editor said, "Nothing ever happened." But at least fifteen townspeople were at the meeting that evening, and their obvious intensity made it feel like twice that amount.

It wasn't the discussion of fire department business that drew the crowd, nor was it the public-service announcement to be given by someone from a U.S. representative's office. In fact, none of the attendees seemed to know that such topics were going to be discussed. They were there for one reason: a rogue bed-and-breakfast was said to be disturbing the peace of an otherwise quiet neighborhood, and they wanted it shut down.

The B&B issue was a complex one for the trustees. They appreciated the business the B&B brought to the township but had to respect the needs of the residents who lived around it. Those residents were in turn certain to find the trustees either tyrannical or ineffective, depending on the evening's decision.

The B&B issue wasn't even taking into consideration the other items on the evening's agenda: the remains of thirty-five bodies from the nineteenth century had recently been discovered in an area of the township cemetery earmarked for new graves. The fire department had answered fifty-eight EMT calls and twenty-four fire incidents over the past two weeks, and the fire chief wanted to buy a new $190,000 ambulance. There was a snow and ice removal conference to attend. Trustees Mucher and Spracklen were up for reelection, and two people in attendance that evening were throwing their names into the race. They attended the meeting proudly, a mild challenge to the incumbent trustees. But such was township business, and so went the trustees' charge.

As 7:00 p.m. approached on September 9, 2015, the crowd filed in and took their seats. Everyone sat rigid and upright, poised to do battle. It would make for an interesting night. The evening was just part of the job of taking care of a small township in southwestern Ohio. It was a township trustee meeting, and one Mucher would shortly call to order.

CHAPTER 1

Quaint Vituperations

The Glen House Inn Controversy

Miami Township trustee Mark Crockett is a man who speaks deliberately, delivering each phrase with the ponderousness of a court justice with all the time in the world. He sat in a judicial posture on the evening of September 9, slightly reclined in his chair behind the table at the head of the room, fingers interlocked over his belly. He looked out on the room with equanimity, observing the proceedings and mulling them over.

Crockett, like the other trustees, was in an interesting position. He and his wife had lived in the area for almost forty years; he owned a business and was a man-about-town who also happened to make important decisions on behalf of his fellow citizens.

Neither Crockett nor any of the other trustees had previous experience holding political office before becoming a township trustee. Spracklen was a farmer, Mucher used to own the area's video rental and film development store, and Crockett was a jeweler and guitar player (though Mucher is an in-law to the DeWine family, an Ohio political dynasty that counts judges, prosecutors, and a state attorney general among its ranks). Trustees picked up civic management skills on the job, and the public had trusted them enough to reelect each of them multiple times.

However, on September 9, Chris Mucher, president of the Miami Township Board of Trustees, warily looked around the meeting room. He could sense tempers were a little high and was concerned

FIGURE 4. Still from the official video of the September 2015 trustee meeting. Trustee Chris Mucher introduces the proceedings. Courtesy of Miami Township.

that the outcome of the evening would likely make some proportionally serious waves. Any decision made was bound to offend someone, and in the case of that evening's meeting, any position the trustees took would offend at least half an entire neighborhood.

The meeting began shortly after 7:00 p.m. Mucher stood up and introduced himself and the rest of the people at the table: fellow trustee Mark Crockett; Margaret Silliman, the financial officer; "number one road employee" Dan Gochenouer; Miami Township zoning inspector Richard Zopf; and Stephanie Hayden, the Greene County assistant prosecutor, who had been called in specifically to give an appraisal of the B&B dispute. Mucher's right hand stayed in the pocket of his khakis as he gave a referee-like preamble to the proceedings. "In our opinion, the board of trustees is the bedrock of local government," he said. "It's the place where the balance begins between the rights of the property owner and the rights of society. Sometimes it gets a little messy, but I assure you tonight isn't going to be messy. It's going to be polite and dignified."

The balance between the rights of the property owner and the rights of society were indeed going to be discussed. The September 9 meeting was the latest battle in an ongoing feud between the Glen House Inn, the B&B in question, and the neighbors it reportedly annoyed. The anti-inn neighbors, the Concerned Circle Citizens (CCC), sat in the front row and nodded. Their de facto spokesperson had brought with her a folder full of stapled documents to prove the soundness of their position. Few people in favor of the B&B were at the meeting, as pains had been taken to avoid telling them the topic was going to be addressed. On the surface, the debate may seem a bit droll: How often does a quaint B&B drive neighbors mad? But such charming disputes are practically written into the township's DNA.

An odd bit of Ohio Code allows the average residential homeowner to run a B&B out of his or her home with little official oversight.[1] A number of area residents, in fact, were taking advantage of this allowance. Miami Township encompasses many picturesque locales, including the village of Yellow Springs, a progressive small town full of art galleries, and a tourist destination most appropriately served by charming B&Bs. A bumper sticker claims the area is "1.3 square miles surrounded by reality," and the area's pastoral vistas suggest this may be the case.

However, as Crockett explained it, most people who lived in Miami Township just wanted to be left alone. A B&B in a quiet neighborhood a few miles outside Yellow Springs was said to be aggressively challenging the desire to live unmolested. The Glen House Inn was accused of hosting dozens of visitors and large-scale events like weddings, self-help workshops, and solstice vigils,

---

1. From the Ohio Revised Code: **5.308 Bed and Breakfast Operations,** under the following conditions: **5.3101** All operations hereunder must meet the definition of Bed and Breakfast. **5.3102** Are operated totally within the principal dwelling and not within a garage or accessory building. **5.3103** Does not have exterior evidence of operation other than one (1) square foot wall sign as permitted under Section 2.14. **5.3104** Shall contain no additional, separate kitchen facilities for guests. **5.3105** Shall provide one (1) off-street parking space for every guest room in addition to the off-street parking otherwise required for the principal structure as provided in each district. **5.3106** Shall permit access to the guest room only through the principal structure. **5.3107** Shall obtain an occupancy permit from Greene County Building Inspection Department prior to the commencement of operations to ensure compliance with all applicable building and safety standards.

a far cry from the romantic (and manageable) couples who usually patronize B&Bs. The excess noise and people "undermined
the quiet integrity of the neighborhood," as one neighbor put it,
and another said he never would have moved to the neighborhood
in the first place had he known the inn would be so loud. Negotia-
tions between the sides had deteriorated—if they were ever civil at
all. Both sides accused the other of being obstinate and dishonest,
and both accused the township of not acting with consistency in
enforcing its laws.

As such, on September 9, the parties sought a definitive interpretation of code. Was the inn operating legally or not? If the inn
were found to be in compliance with Ohio law, the neighbors
would just have to deal with it; should the inn be found in violation, the B&B would have to scale back its operations, a change
the inn's owner said would ruin him financially.

Prosecutor Hayden was there to give an official interpretation of the law and to offer suggestions about what steps could
be taken to square everything with code. Throughout the meeting,
her face held a look of intelligent skepticism, the look of someone
professionally capable of seeing through bullshit.

The crowd murmured, eager to get started. Richard Zopf, the
wild-bearded township zoning inspector, appeared to be trying to
relax while knowing that the whole room was eager to blame him
for their troubles. Gochenouer, the road crewman and cemetery
sexton whose official business didn't have anything to do with the
crowd, folded his hands and faintly smiled.

Genesis of the Dispute

Glen Drive, where the Glen House Inn was then located, is a ten-
minute drive from the Miami Township Fire and Rescue (MTFR)
building. Down Corry Street, past a nature preserve and a stable
of therapeutic horses, is Grinnell Road. A left turn on Grinnell
takes the visitor down a sizable hill and onto a road overlooked
by the colorful buildings of a wastewater treatment facility. A few
miles further south, the visitor will come to a noticeably bucolic
setting, a clearing with stone walls and an old mill with a water-

FIGURE 5. Entrance to the Glen House Inn as seen from Glen Circle. The B&B is the first house on the left when you come into the Glen Circle neighborhood from Grinnell Road. Photo by Dylan Taylor-Lehman.

wheel set among hedges and trees. Glen Drive and the Glen Circle neighborhood are nestled back in this splendiferous idyll.

Glen Circle is a collection of homesteads grouped around an acre of common area. Some neighbors have gates, others none; most have a decent amount of money. Erik and Deirdre Owen, the owners of the inn, spent $700,000 to build a large house on the circle in 2005, largely because of the circle's regal charm. Both grew up in Yellow Springs and wanted to return to its friendly community. Their house was based on a dream home they had sketched on a cocktail napkin in Europe many years before.

When the dispute began, Erik was in his late 40s, thickset, and unkempt in a way that bespeaks of his consistent productivity in his pursuits. He was a kind of wheeler-dealer, active in the art world and owner of a few properties, including part of a hotel in a small town in Michigan. He was thrust into bed-and-breakfast ownership when he had a falling-out with the partners of a company he had founded twenty-five years before. He took a year's salary and retired but quickly recognized the money was not enough to sustain him forever. A beautiful house was at his disposal, and, knowing of the allowances in code, he decided to turn it into a B&B. The

FIGURE 6. View of the Glen Circle Center Commons as seen as you drive into the neighborhood. Photo by Dylan Taylor-Lehman.

Glen House Inn's website was up and running within thirty days of his decision. He said it was the only way to save the house.

The Owens were also confident they had done a good thing for the area. The home was not only an impressive place to stay but an impressive art gallery. "Yellow Springs is a good place because it already has cachet, and people expect art and eccentricity," Deirdre said at the time. "It's what our house was always meant to be," Erik added.

In the interest of being open about his plans, and in order to get a permit to follow through with them, Owen met with the Board of Zoning Appeals in July 2011. The BZA overhears building plans, checks them against zoning code, and questions prospective builders about the effects the construction will have on the surroundings. All BZA meetings are open to the public, and citizens are encouraged to attend to weigh in with their concerns. Anti-inn neighbors came to the BZA meeting, anticipating that the B&B would create trouble, and they wanted to register their concerns right away.

Both sides granted that some kind of tenuous agreement was reached regarding the operations of the inn, but none of the claims about what was said can be proven, as the official record for this meeting has disappeared. Video of any BZA meeting would ordi-

FIGURE 7. View of the other side of the commons, looking toward the Glen House Inn. Photo by Dylan Taylor-Lehman.

narily be available through the local cable access station or on a DVD at the library, but the master recording could no longer be found, and the person who took notes at the meeting no longer worked for the township. Ultimately, Zopf recalled, "there was no reason not to grant Owen a permit," as Owen's plans seemed reasonable and legally kosher.

With the impression everything was on the up-and-up, the Owens opened the Glen House Inn. Guests lined up to rent its five spacious rooms, lounge on its patio, appreciate the impressive art collection, and swim in its stream-fed pool. The whole inn was bathed in the tranquil, sunlit green characteristic of eighteenth-century paintings. It was an objectively beautiful location, and business was steady.

However, perhaps because of the bacchanalia that some such locations induce, neighbors said their concerns about disturbed peace were immediately proven to be valid. Catering trucks parked on the berm of the already-narrow road. Fireworks—"nice ones, like you'd see in town"—were said to have almost hit two houses at 12:45 a.m. Guests playing in the pool were too noisy. One resident said he was unhappy with unknown people lurking in the neighborhood, and he described a recent occurrence in which a car circled around the neighborhood before parking at the inn.

"Why would they do that?" he asked. "I think it's a safety concern."

(The Owens maintained that some of these events happened once and never again and that the neighbors have been referencing the same events for years. And people drive on the road, Owen said, because it's a public road.)

The neighbors maintained that they had complained to the township and the county about the B&B, to no avail, for at least four years. But in 2015, action was taken after the inn's broken septic system began stinking up the area. The ghastly effluence was definitely coming from the inn, one neighbor said: "A lot of sniff-testing confirmed it." The Greene County Health Department investigated—they have jurisdiction over septic systems—and deemed the septic system completely inadequate for the number of people the inn hosted.

By this point the Owens had moved back to Michigan, and the operations of the inn were being managed by live-in caretaker Jody Farrar and her husband Bill. The Owens and Farrars conceded the septic system was not working and fixed it. Other repairs were undertaken, and the inn continued hosting guests and renting out their facilities at a rate of $5,000 per weekend. The noise was alleged to have continued unabated.

The final straw was when neighbors got wind that Owen was talking about reworking the property into a winery. It was a clever power play, they said, as viticulture is exempt from zoning. A winery is considered an agricultural practice, and Ohio Code is oddly explicit in noting that townships have no jurisdiction over them, including a say-so in the zoning of buildings as part of the agricultural operation.[2]

---

2. From the Ohio Revised Code: **519.21 Powers not conferred on township zoning commission by chapter:** Except as otherwise provided in division (B) and (D) of this section, sections 519.02 to 519.25 of the Revised Code confer no power on any township zoning commission, board of township trustees, or board of zoning appeals to prohibit the use of any land for agricultural purposes or the construction or use of buildings or structures incident to the use for agricultural purposes of the land on which such buildings or structures are located, including buildings or structures that are used primarily for vinting and selling wine and that are located on land any part of which is used for viticulture, and no zoning certificate shall be required for any such building or structure.

Section B, which the above references, includes exceptions such as a parcel of land of five acres or less or one located in a platted subdivision containing

Owen had no qualms using viticulture as leverage. "I'll convert it to a winery rather than face foreclosure," he said. "Then there'll be hundreds of cars per weekend versus just a few." (When the viticulture possibility was brought up at the meeting on September 9, Stephanie Hayden wasn't impressed. "We have a lot of people threaten to open a winery to get zoning off their back," she said.)

Credible threat or not, the neighbors ramped up their efforts to get the township to intervene, hence the invitation to Hayden to attend the meeting and the CCC's eager faces in the front row.

At the Meeting of September 9, 2015

September 9 was it—the neighbors' big meeting, their big chance for an official showdown. The anti-inn neighbors were sober and ready to go; partners held hands for encouragement. After Mucher's brief opening speech ("the bedrock of local government," etc.), he introduced Hayden.

Hayden was Greene County's prosecutor, and, by statute, the township's lawyer, she said.[3] She began by clearly and concisely explaining what roles the various boards and commissions played in the B&B drama. She outlined the process of suing someone over zoning concerns, the difference between civil and municipal court, and the possible outcomes of such a suit ($500 per day per violation, in one instance). Her elucidations were illustrated with examples of other problematic zoning cases. "One guy was a junk property owner, an outdoor hoarder. We disagree on what the definition of 'junk' is," she said.

She then asked the neighbors to present their case.

"When did these problems start?" Hayden asked.

"First of June, 2011," said the head of the CCC immediately.

Her ready answer prompted laughs.

---

fifteen or more lots. On a lot that is one acre or smaller, zoning may prohibit or regulate all agricultural activities.

3. A state law passed in 1999 allowed Ohio townships to be represented by their respective county's county prosecutor. Previously, county prosecutors could represent individual township officials should they be accused of wrongdoing but could not represent the township as an entity. If the township were taken to court, the township would have had borne the cost of hiring legal protection. Since the law was passed, however, townships are afforded the same legal help as any other local, county, and state jurisdictions. This information was courtesy of Chris Mucher.

"We're on top of this," the neighbor said.

The CCC enumerated the violations and complaints that plagued the inn since it had opened. Not only was the inn hosting many more guests than it was legally allowed, the CCC spokesperson argued, but the Owens didn't even live in Ohio, which meant that the inn wasn't owner-occupied, which meant that it wasn't even technically in line with code.

Hayden listened to the neighbors' complaints with total concentration, her body involuntarily twitching when she heard a particularly egregious violation. The neighbors were very thorough in their overview. "You're the best witnesses I've ever had," Hayden said. Her assessment was obvious: the parameters of what is officially acceptable for B&Bs, as well as parameters of any other official regulations used by a county or city agency, are plainly spelled out in the Ohio Revised Code, the Ohio Administrative Code, and the Miami Township Code. These laws are indisputable, and she was clearly baffled that the inn was still in operation at all. Her expression also hinted at her feelings as a human being annoyed by other humans who think they're special.

All things considered, Hayden said, it made sense to convene representatives from all agencies involved in the dispute and file a formal complaint against the inn. She suggested giving the inn a "fill-in-the-blanks violation of notice," a predrafted letter the agencies could just fill in with the violations they would inevitably discover. Official procedure was to ask the violating entity to fix these violations or be shut down. Hayden and Zopf agreed that they would pay the inn a visit in a few days. The trustees sat back in their chairs with evident relief. A decision needed to be made, and it was.

With this decision reached, about 98 percent of the people at the meeting gathered their belongings and got up to leave. "You're welcome to stay for the rest of the . . . ," Mucher began, but the attendees filed past him and went straight back outside. Snatches of their conversation could be heard as the door swung open and closed. The first part of the September 9 meeting had taken one hour and fourteen seconds.

A Visit to the Inn

The Glen House Inn was apparently subject to intimidation in the days following the meeting. According to Erik Owen, someone pounded on the door in the middle of the night, and guests reported what sounded like guns being shot off right next to the house.

Things did not improve from there. Five days after the trustee meeting, on September 14, a contingent of county and township functionaries paid the inn a visit. The Owens traveled down from Michigan to lead the zoning- and health-code inspectors on what they thought was a "fact-finding mission" to determine what aspects of the inn needed to be brought up to code. Instead, Owen said, they were surprised to find themselves served with a cease-and-desist letter, just as Hayden had suggested.

The letter said the inn had two weeks from that day to scale back its operations or it would be shut down. The inn could have no more than five guests in its current incarnation, the letter said, and it could not host any events. It also had to stop its activities as an art gallery (or venue of any kind), as it also violated statutes defining what constitutes a home-based business.

Erik Owen promptly called the *Yellow Springs News,* as he knew that a reporter was at the September 9 trustee meeting and wanted to provide the world with this shocking update. He and Deirdre and the Farrars and his mother Luisa were sitting outside on deck chairs when the reporter arrived, astounded by the morning's events. Owen related what happened with the impassioned but disjointed cadence of someone thinking aloud. After a few minutes he paused and held out a lit cigarette.

"Look what they have me doing," he said. "I don't even smoke."

The agencies' letter effectively meant he would have to turn the B&B into a hotel, Owen said. In order for the inn to host the number of guests it had been hosting, Owen would have to install steel doors, fire dampeners, hood systems in the kitchen, and a 150,000-gallon cistern for a sprinkler system in his house. It was an expense he simply could not afford.

The CCC was basically a "lynch mob" that had their "tentacles" in county and township agencies, he said. This was nothing like the community he used to know. He said Greene County authorities were toadies following the regulations created by and directly benefitting the worldwide hotel industry. Owen's mother compared the inn's situation with the policies of the fascist regime she lived through as a young woman in a prison camp in Yugoslavia.

"Where I grew up, they would kill you for speaking up. If that were the case here, I would still speak up about the inn," she said.

But the caretakers nonetheless got to work making two of the five rooms unavailable. They had to remove an illegal downstairs bathroom and take out some beds as a show of good faith that they wouldn't secretly accommodate more guests than they were allowed. Jody Farrar said she had to call and tell people they couldn't have their wedding at the inn. The guests went from angry to devastated, she said, as some people had already ordered decorations specifically to go with the property—all of this, Owen said, after the largesse the inn had shown the area, like the free use of the inn for area cultural affairs and "at least 50 meals and $400 in wine purchased in town" by guests of a recent event.

They would just have to wait and see if the inn would still be sustainable.

The Second Meeting—September 21, 2015

Tempers ran high at the subsequent trustees meeting two weeks later. If the September 9 meeting was noteworthy for its attendance, this one was exceptional. Supporters of the inn said it was their duty to show up and testify on the inn's behalf, as they had deliberately been excluded from the previous meeting. The CCC was there to advocate again for their position.

The trustees filed in from the corridor. Trustee Lamar Spracklen wasn't at the previous meeting, but he was this time. He sat down in his chair and stared out at the room. He looked like a grizzled boxing instructor who commands someone to punch a side of meat, and he had a bandage on his face that stretched from his lip to his cheekbone. His eyes scanned the crowd, like he was just waiting for someone to ask why it was there. Gochenouer was at the table, and so were Crockett, Silliman, and Zopf.

Chris Mucher stood up and with little official preamble addressed the crowd. There was a slight tremble in his voice.

"If anyone thinks they're in the wrong place, they're not," he said. "This is exactly where you want to be. This is a public meeting of the Board of Trustees."

The inn's supporters were ready to go. A neighbor named Dan Rudolf spoke, lauding the operations of the inn and saying he was not bothered by the occasional noise. His speech was delivered

FIGURE 8. Trustee Chris Mucher. Photo courtesy of the *Yellow Springs News*.

with an eloquence that bespoke serious conviction, or at least a great deal of time spent rehearsing its delivery. Innkeeper Bill Farrar, tall, with a wispy red beard and long red ponytail, stood up and added his piece. He tried to make the difficult argument that the neighbors were being un-neighborly—a subjective characteristic that was hard to objectively prove and a point that was difficult to understand because his speech was peppered with phrases like "maybe it's not your job to promote community" and "losing the opportunity to eat potato salad with the Lithgows,"[4] on top of referring to the official proceedings as a "plot." By the looks on the faces of the other attendees, the strength of his case was dampened by the profligate use of these rhetorical illustrations.

Owen's eyes were sparkling with a barely containable desire to speak. He leapt up. Did the township know the position he and Deirdre were being put in? he asked.

---

4. Sometimes the inn was rented out by Antioch College as a home for its special guests, which once included actor John Lithgow and his family. Lithgow's father was a theater professor at Antioch, and John Lithgow had attended daycare in Yellow Springs.

"We're basically vagabonds," he said. "We have no house; we sleep when there are free rooms in the bed and breakfast." He already worked eighteen hours a day, he said, and now he had to deal with this.

"If the neighbors wanted a gated community, why don't they just create a gated community?" he asked.

He wasn't inherently opposed to code, he said, and every time he was asked, he tried to square his property with it. But the changes the inn had to make were difficult to understand, thanks to the unclear information given by the township and the fact that county and Ohio codes didn't always line up. It was tough to tell which code took precedence, he said. Either way, he felt the inn was being ganged up on.

"I don't know what club you're part of," Owen said.

"I don't have a club," said Mucher. "This has absolutely nothing to do with any other department or political subdivision."

"I mean the club we're being beaten with," Owen replied.

More testimony was heard from Bob Bingenheimer, whose letter to the editor, originally titled "Glen House Closing Shows Worst of People and Government," was published in the paper earlier that week, though its title was changed to something less acerbic. Another innkeeper in town offered her take on the issue, arguing against the necessity of strictly following the owner-occupancy requirement for small-scale B&Bs.

Here, trustee Spracklen weighed in. He sympathized with the Owens and told of his own troubles running his own B&B. He was the owner-operator of another picturesque area inn, and his B&B necessarily operated under the same township code. Spracklen's establishment had recently come under fire for serving a number of meals far too large for its permit, and he sarcastically explained how the Health Department demanded significant upgrades to the kitchen.

"Don't make me laugh or my tape'll fall off," he said, touching his bandage. (A few weeks later he would basically be in Owen's position, pleading his case to the Health Department.)

The CCC was there and pleaded their case anew, going point-for-point with Owen's. The argument got more convoluted as more people weighed in. There was a circuitous discussion of what defines traffic on the circle, followed by a discussion on the nature of socializing itself. Mucher stepped in and gave a ten-minute warning, mentioning as he had at the first meeting that no real or enforceable resolution would be coming from this meeting, or the next one, or any future meetings. A change to the zoning code required advocating for the change before the Zoning Commission, who would render their expert opinion and eventually suggest a change for the trustees to vote on.

The public debate portion of the September 21 meeting ran for the next ten minutes, and then the trustees wrapped it up. There was not much more to say and little that could be done at that moment. The attendees once again got up and left as soon as the debate session was over, the two sides avoiding further interaction and leaving the building to fume in private.

Ultimately, the case added up to this: because the Owens had more than five guests, because it was shown that the Owens were registered taxpayers in Michigan, because the property was zoned residential, and because they didn't have the appropriate health, fire, and food licenses, the Glen House Inn would have to limit, in perpetuity, its B&B operations to those allowed in residentially zoned properties. The mandates of the letter signed jointly by the Greene County Combined Health District and the Miami Township offices were not up for debate—code was there for a reason, and that reason could not be selectively enforced, no matter how fascistic or unfair it may have seemed. There had to be some structure, and that structure was outlined in Miami Township Code.

"That's the most dramatic thing about being a trustee—whether you like it or not, changes happen," Crockett said. "Our job is to try to make the best decision for the majority of the people in the community."

A decision had been reached on September 14. The cease-and-desist letter spelled out what the inn had to do, and the requirements of the letter stood.

So What Happened with the Glen House B&B?

As can be expected with an issue this contentious, the ruling did not go over well. Almost every party felt wronged in some way, and those feelings did not necessarily diminish over time because it is simply difficult to get over the feeling of having been insulted.

The inn reduced its operations within the fourteen days demanded by the letter and stayed at that level through the following spring. Its available rooms were consistently booked. The inn was allowed to stay open because it was determined that the Owens did have residency in Ohio, as the inn was their registered address and Ohio law does not specify a length of time required for residency.

An article about this controversy was published in the *Yellow Springs News* not long after the second Board of Trustees meeting. The article presented an overview of the debate and reported on the cease-and-desist letter, suggesting that the inn was shut down as a result. Zoning inspector Richard Zopf was quick to point out that this was not the case. He wrote a letter to the editor that said the article made his office look bad and had misinterpreted the township's position. The inn was not closed down, he pointed out; it just had to stop its violations. He maintained that this was his position all along—all the suggestions he had ever given, all the leniency he had shown the Owens—were in the interest of getting the inn in compliance with code. He, in his duty as zoning inspector, was simply trying to follow the letter of the law. He admitted he had been lenient in the time he allowed residents to comply, but he no longer would be. He had been taken advantage of by both sides, he said, and from that point on was going to be strict in his definitions of what was acceptable and what was not.

Jody Farrar said it seemed like the authorities were trying to cover their tracks in going after the inn. There are five B&Bs in the area, she said, but the inn was "dissected" because the Health Department realized they were supposed to be monitoring B&Bs but weren't, and the department went after one of them in order to save face. Bill Farrar, speaking with his customary grandiloquence, said "The shrapnel rained down and gave us all paper cuts; we didn't die but we were severely injured." Owen said members of the CCC had called them and pretended to be someone looking to book an event to see if the inn would slip up.

In late March 2016, a pro-inn neighbor wrote a letter to the editor stating that she wished to be published in the *Yellow Springs News*. Titled "Unintended Consequences: An Essay about Community, a Cautionary Tale," it decried the township's decision, saying that all semblance of neighborly cooperation had been bulldozed by the CCC's intractable opposition to the Owens.

The letter ran many thousands of words, and the editor of the *Yellow Springs News* said it had to be cut by at least 75 percent to be published. The author said she couldn't do this, as the argument had to be presented in its entirety. She actually increased the length of the essay and said she was willing to pay $800 to run it as a full-page ad. A mock-up of the full-page version of the essay looked disarmingly like the screed of a political radical. The staff of the news were unsure if they wanted to open the paper up to that kind of self-expression.

Initially, Owen asked the well-intentioned neighbor not to go through with publishing her lengthy missive. He had a prospective buyer for the property and didn't want to dredge up problems associated with the house. However, he relented, and the neighbor published the letter as a half-page ad on the back page of the news. Not long after, in summer 2016, the house was sold and reverted back to its first incarnation as a private residence. According to Owen, it just wasn't worth it to keep the Glen House Inn going. "I've dealt with this same provincial shit before with my hotel in Michigan," Owen said, "but this was something else."[5]

---

5. "Unintended Consequences" is included in its entirety as Appendix A.

A Brief History of Miami Township's Boundaries, Development, and the People Therein

When the door swung closed behind the last debater leaving the September 9 meeting, the only people left in the meeting room were the township trustees and other officials as well as Marty Heide, Zo Van Eaton-Meister, and Dale Amstutz. The latter two were there to remind people—and the other trustees—that they were going to be running for trustee office in November. Amstutz reportedly had a bone to pick with Spracklen and seemed pleased with the fact that he was there but Spracklen wasn't.

All in all, the Glen House Inn fracas proved to be a unique case for the trustees. It wasn't often that cases like that came before the board, Mucher said, though he mentioned that the township had recently heard another case testing the limits of residential zoning, one involving a homeowner said to be hosting "commercial truck pulling activities" on his property attended by "hundreds of people."

But that part of the meeting was over. After a quick breather and an exchange of relieved looks, it was time to move on to the rest of the evening's business.

Marty Heide stood up and introduced herself. "Thanks for an entertaining meeting," she said. Heide was an attaché for U.S. Representative Mike Turner's office, who represents Ohio's 10th District. She was making her way around southwestern Ohio and explaining to local governments and civic groups the services offered by the representative's office. She was at the September 9 trustees meeting specifically to speak about how the senator could expedite the passport renewal process.

"You have to have a passport to go anywhere," she said. "If you want to go fishing in Canada, you're not coming back without a passport."

If a person's passport renewal process is taking longer than he has time for, Turner's office could be contacted to look into the status of the passport and push it through to completion. Instead of the six-week turnaround estimated by the U.S. passport agency, Heide said, she could help get a passport in as little as ten days. It was politicking of the old-school variety: direct contact with representatives yields results.

Heide finished her brief announcement and bid everyone farewell. She had to make the same announcement elsewhere that evening. That was her job—a tireless public relations apparatchik. She told everyone not to hesitate in getting in touch with the senator's office for a favor.

"I always tell people, 'use us and abuse us,'" she said.

Hayden remarked with genuine awe that she sees Heide at meetings everywhere.

"Thanks for all you do," Hayden told her.

Although Mucher had begun the evening with a brief speech, it was intended to be only a prologue to the discussion with the B&B group and didn't officially open the September 9 meeting. Protocol had to be followed, and that included calling the meeting to order, adopting the previous minutes, and making a motion to approve the payment of bills, which, at this meeting, amounted to $68,854.94. The officials went through the (literal) motions quickly, with Silliman pausing to only briefly to explain what bills were being paid. With items (1), (2), and (3) on the agenda taken care of, the meeting was officially underway. The trustees could get to work as the nerve center and strategic headquarters of Miami Township.

What Is a Township Exactly, and How Does It Work?

As long as there has been a township, there have been people to help run it, and the trustees have been part of a tradition that dates back almost two hundred years. That evening's business, with its impassioned zoning concerns, is one of the many ways in which township residents have defined the word *community*.

Miami Township was founded on June 6, 1808, a land of verdant beauty bisected north to south by the meandering Little Miami River. Miami Township is one of five townships in Ohio bearing that name, another of which is less than twenty miles away.[6] (Ohio also has a Miami County.) Ohio has 1,309 townships ranging in size from a few hundred to tens of thousands of residents. About half of the state's 11.5 million residents live in these jurisdictions.

Townships are subdivisions of counties, with powers of self-government delegated by the state. Three trustees and a financial officer (previously known as a clerk) oversee every aspect of a township's operations. The powers they are accorded are multifaceted and are outlined in the Ohio Revised Code. In one capacity, they function like administrators and manage the day-to-day operations of the township, but they can also create or amend laws if they need to, a laborious process that can involve public hearings and the recommendations of myriad committees. However, unlike municipal governments, which can write laws mandating changes specific to the needs of that community, Ohio townships can do only what the state statutorily allows.

---

6. There are apparently no rules governing the naming of Ohio townships. Five Miami Townships are nothing compared to Ohio's ten Adams Townships, twenty-six Perry Townships, six Sugarcreek Townships, twenty-seven Union Townships, twenty-one Wayne Townships, and an astonishing forty-three Washington Townships.

And not all Miami Townships are financially equal. The Miami Township closest to Greene County's Miami Township is located in Montgomery County and is a suburb of Dayton. This Miami Township is faced with similar administrative concerns but on a significantly larger scale: its officials negotiate $30 million construction projects, enter into negotiations with huge waste-management firms, zone land for megamalls, and have had a public relations firm help with its branding efforts. This same township also had to deal with an explosion at a biochemical facility on September 1, 2003. Firefighters and personnel at Isotec/Sigma Aldrich were fixing a nitric oxide leak when an explosion occurred, blowing off part of the roof and injuring one worker. (Normally inflammable, nitric oxide can explode when jostled. The explosion was likely either from a heater that collapsed under pressure, or the boiling of the gas as it escaped at high velocity.) Nobody else was in the plant at the time, and more than 2,000 nearby residents were evacuated in case of a second explosion.

But while Ohio townships can't do something such as legislate that all houses be painted green (as Ohio Code doesn't explicitly say they can), township officials *do* have the authority to create parks and open a township police department; they can regulate mining on township land and can establish landfills. Trustees can adjust parking policy and levy taxes with resident approval. In short, they administer almost everything the township needs to keep functioning.

In Ohio, township residents in both incorporated and unincorporated areas of the township[7] vote for township trustees. All officials are elected to four-year terms, and all trustee elections take place in odd-numbered years. Two of the candidate seats are voted on in one cycle (quadrennially from 1949), and the other seat in a separate cycle (from 1951). Township operations and services are funded by local property taxes and money from the state. The county government approves the township's budget.

All told, as of a survey conducted in 2012, there are 16,360 township governments across twenty states, which are classified by the U.S. Census Bureau as Minor Civil Divisions. (In contrast, there are 19,519 municipal governments in the United States.) Not all townships are governed the same way. The respective amount of autonomy depends on the state.

Some township forms of government are called by names other than *township*. Some states use *town, grant, purchase,* or the simple catchall *location.* In North Carolina, some counties have started naming their townships numerically—for example, "Township 8"—instead of endowing them with a proper noun, while Minnesota state law holds that township names must be in the form "_____ Township." In eleven of the twenty states, townships are present in all county-type areas and overlapping municipalities. In five states, townships are the only kind of territory other

---

7. An incorporated area, like a city or village, exists within a township but governs itself independently. Residents of Yellow Springs and Clifton, the two incorporated villages in Miami Township, are residents of both that village and the township, while people who live outside these areas are citizens of the township only. Yellow Springers can vote for candidates filling both village and township offices, but people who live in unincorporated areas of the township can vote only for township trustees. If the boundaries of an incorporated area expand to become equal to those of the township it's in, the authority of the incorporated city or town trumps that of the township, and the township and its government are dissolved.

than municipalities, aside from what is called *unorganized territories,* which have no local government but are overseen by larger state authorities.

The term *township* itself is a holdover from what used to be called a *survey township,* a six-by-six-mile plot divided into thirty-six sections of 640 acres each. (Technically, in the sense of the word as it is used today, townships are called *civil townships,* to distinguish them from survey townships.) The Midwest was settled largely by dividing the land into these townships, divisions that eventually gave rise to incorporated cities and towns. "No other feature so marks the Midwestern landscape as the signature of townships," writes Michael Martone in *Townships,* a book about the history of townships. Indeed, of the states that have townships, none are farther west than the Dakotas or farther southwest than Kansas.

Tracing the Township's History and Its Earliest Settlers

Most of Miami Township is rural and fairly flat, the result of being squashed by the glacier that covered most of Ohio as recently as 14,000 years ago. Glaciers leveled almost everything but the southeastern quarter of the state, leaving mostly flat, scoured landscapes in its wake. The area features a number of massive boulders in unexpected places, huge chunks of stone picked up by the glacier, suspended in ice, and then deposited on the ground as the glaciers retreated. Miami Township is regarded as one of the most fertile townships in the area, with soils made healthy thanks to the many area springs.

The name *Miami* was the name given to an indigenous group who lived in the area and is said to mean "people from downstream." The Miami, as Europeans called them, came up from the Mississippi River area and spread from the middle of Indiana up to the Great Lakes around the time Europeans were exploring Ohio. But indigenous groups had lived in Ohio for at least 12,000 years. Around 1700 BCE, a seminomadic group collectively called the Adena culture lived in an area spreading from southern Ohio to Indiana, Kentucky, and West Virginia. (The name *Adena* is a term of "archaeological convenience" that encompasses a culture whose name or language is unknown.) The Adena people belonging to the Adena culture are also known as *mound builders* after the earthworks they constructed. The mounds, often enclosed by an earthen ring, were used for burial purposes. Miami Township hosts four mounds, one circle mound, and one single burial. A famous mound in Yellow Springs was co-opted by settlers and named "Orators Mound," as speakers used to stand on it to deliver their harangues. At one point, listeners were moved by the eloquence of Henry Clay, Daniel Webster, and Martin Van Buren.

The Adena peoples disappeared or dispersed for unknown reasons and were followed by a culture collectively called the *Hopewell*, which arose around 100 BCE. The group was said to be characterized by their complex trading routes and advanced pottery, and they too built earthworks but on a larger and often more grandiose scale. Their mounds are massive representations of animals and geometric shapes and are filled with a variety of artifacts. This culture declined around 400 AD, likewise for reasons unknown. Over the centuries, various other indigenous groups passed through or made permanent homes in the area. The Shawnees had two well-known settlements to the north and south of what would become Miami Township. The famous Shawnee chief Tecumseh was born in Mad River Village, the settlement six miles to the north. White settlers had forcibly removed most native peoples from the area by the mid-1800s.

Ohio became a state in 1803, the seventeenth in the union, though settlers had been in the area for decades, trapping game and fighting with indigenous groups. In an attempt to alleviate the debt stemming from the Revolutionary War, the U.S. government sold off parts of the Northwest Territory, which encompassed land stretching from Ohio to Michigan to parts of Wisconsin and Minnesota. One of the original subdivisions of Ohio land was the Virginia Military District, more than 6,500 square miles of land reserved for those who had served in the Revolutionary War. Higher rank and length of service granted soldiers a larger tract. Many people took advantage of this promise of land and moved to the state. Settlements and provisional governments were set up, creating a population of around 40,000 by the time statehood was being considered. Although laws for statehood at the time required a minimum of 60,000 citizens, lawmakers assumed the population would increase and so jump-started the process. Statehood was officially declared on February 9, 1803, though an official resolution saying as much slipped through the cracks. To fix this, in 1953 President Eisenhower, in a retroactive inauguration, declared Ohio's official founding as March 1, 1803, and said that "the 150-year lapse in formal admittance did not affect Ohio's legal status as a state."

Greene County, the county in which Miami Township is located, was likewise established in 1803 and named for a general in the Revolutionary War. "It is a source of regret that more care has not been taken to preserve the history of the early settlers of the County of Greene," wrote historian George F. Robinson in 1897. It is thanks in part to Robinson that much of the county's history is known. Robinson realized that many of the area's founding documents were in the unsorted boxes stashed in the attics of government buildings around Greene County, "like a well-worn garment cast away." He took it upon himself to sort through these documents and preserve what history he could. He even managed to get a weekly salary from a government agency to do so. He compiled his findings in a 1902 book titled, remarkably, *Robinson's History of Greene County: Embracing the Organization of the County, Its Division into Townships, Sketches of Local Interest Gleaned from the Pioneers from 1803 to 1840, Together with a Roster of the Soldiers of the Revolution and the War of 1812, Who Were Residing in the County, also, A Roster of Ten Thousand of the Early Settlers from 1803 to 1840.*

Officials began organizing Greene County into townships in 1803; their headquarters were a log cabin residence/courthouse[8]

---

8. As there was apparently not much official business to be done at the courthouse, one resident recalled that "doubtless thought it a great pity to have a learned court and nothing for it to do, so they set to and cut out employment for their honors by engaging in divers[e] hard fights at fisticuffs, right on the ground. So it seems our pioneers fought for the benefit of the court. At all events, while their honors were waiting to settle differences according to law, they were making up issues and settling them by trial '*by combat*'—a process by which they avoided the much complained of 'law's delay,' and incurred no other damages than black eyes and bloody noses, which were regarded as mere trifles, of course."

A man named Owen Davis charged another with "speculating in pork," or stealing his neighbor's hogs. "The insult was resented—a combat took place forthwith in which Davis proved victorious. He then went into court, and, planting himself in front of the judges, he observed, addressing himself particularly to one of them, 'Well, Ben, I've whipped that d—d hog-thief—what's the damage? What's to pay?' and thereupon, suiting the action to the word, he drew out his five miles west of Xenia. At the time, the county was "almost an entire wilderness—a primeval forest, planted by the hand of nature" with settlements so far apart that "the traveler might find one of these primitive dwellings sending up its smoke from a mud and stick chimney among the giants of the forest, each cabin with a little patch of a corn-field, thickly dotted over with girdled trees." The area was full of game, and crops grew abundantly.

Both the township and the county were originally much bigger than they currently are: at one point, Greene County stretched all the way to the top of Ohio. But their square mileage was reduced when county boundaries were redrawn no less than three times over the succeeding decade. Ross, Vance, and Clark counties usurped part of northern Greene County, which reduced the township down to its current size.

The boundary change in 1818 bounced the property of one Greene County man's property into Clark County. The man, a "noted [and] daring Indian fighter" named General Benjamin Whiteman, was miffed at this geographic slight. Whiteman, who "possessed very large ears, which seem to have served him well among the Indians and guided him through a strenuous but successful life," made such a stink about changing counties that he was able to have a bill introduced into the Ohio General Assembly in 1819 that specifically redrew his property back into Greene County.[9]

A few individuals are said to hold the distinction of being the township's first permanent (white) settler, but a man named Lewis Davis is the most-agreed-upon candidate. Davis, who happened to be the brother-in-law of the cantankerous General Whiteman, was "frequently engaged in surveying land" and accumulated considerable property. He founded a few towns in the area and moved

---

buckskin purse . . . and slammed it down on the table—then shaking his fist at the judge . . . he continued 'Yes, Ben, and if you'd steal a hog, d—n you, I'd whip you too.'" Davis was fined eight dollars for the fight (Howe, vol. 1, p. 695).

9. Whiteman, "in conversation, was not an employer of the first person. He never had much to say of his experience with Indians, but, to stop the questions of an inquisitive boy, would sometimes tell an Indian story. He would never admit that he had ever killed an Indian. However once he did say that while seeking a crossing, he saw what was apparently an empty canoe floating down the river. With caution he swam to the canoes and as he grabbed its bow an Indian raised up with tomahawk lifted. In this instance, he did say he paddled the canoe to shore" (McCullough, p. 4–5).

permanently to Ohio after selling wholesale a town he owned in Indiana. A chance meeting with an "Indian maid" in 1799 led to him to the land that would ultimately become Miami Township. The woman "who, for some reason, struck up an acquaintance with him," told him of a beautiful nearby land full of forests, fields, and springs. Davis went to check it out and was so impressed that he promptly surveyed the land and purchased it from the state congress in 1803. "Davis is not said to have married the girl, although it would have added flavor to the story if he had," notes historian Michael A. Broadstone in his 1918 *History of Greene County, Ohio*. Davis built a tavern, traded with the Shawnee, and eventually marketed water from what was called the area's "yellow springs," noting in an advertisement that the area's "air and water are esteemed particularly salubrious." The rocks where the springs flow are colored yellow by the water's iron content—hence the name for the springs and the town that was built up around them.

The springs were said to be the meeting place of different tribes, a sort of rejuvenating way station for settlers and Native Americans passing through the area. The water comes from deep underground, and as a result the water is the same temperature all year round. In addition, the springs' 110-gallon-per-minute output is not affected by drought or flood. At one point, a caravan of Shawnee stopped at the spring on a fifteen-day walk to Detroit with a captive Daniel Boone.[10]

Lewis Davis appears to have left the township area sometime around 1811, bouncing around other counties and states and making a fairly comfortable living as a land surveyor. Davis "seemed to have been a man of some ability," but he "fell prey to the wiles of King Alcohol" (or, as another historian put it, "he preferred corn in the liquid form to the product in the shape of meal"). He fell into ruin, dying in obscurity. "His career from 1817 until his death is shrouded in mystery," and a few decades later an

---

10. An area colonel recalled meeting Boone when Boone was around sixty years old, when they both stayed for a few nights at the same house. The colonel said Boone was "medium size . . . not given to corpulency, retired, unobtrusive, and a man of few words. . . . I well remember his dress was of tow cloth, and not a woolen garment on his body, unless his stockings were of that material. Home-made was the common wear of the people of Kentucky, at that time: sheep were not yet introduced into the country" (Howe, vol. 1, p. 693–94).

anonymous writer said Davis was buried under a large boulder in northwestern Logan County. The writer penned a quick eulogy for the man, remarking that Davis died "unhonored, unwept, and unknown." (Lewis Davis's son, Claiborne, also suffered a forgotten death as well. Using pseudonyms, he and some friends enlisted in the Mexican-American War in 1846. He contracted an exotic fever and died when he returned home, his final resting place noted with a small, unmarked stone.)

But slowly Miami Township grew, boasting ninety-six tax-paying citizens in 1808 and a handful of squatters. (In fact, the first squatter was a man who will please fans of *The Office*: Sebastian Schroufe, who came from Germany with his large family.) Anna, born in 1804, was the first girl born in the established township, the daughter of Mary and John Graham, who came to the area to "start a fireside of [their] own." By 1820, a census indicated that 579 people were living in the township.

On Clifton and Yellow Springs

Miami Township currently boasts around 5,000 residents, approximately 3,000 of whom live in Yellow Springs and 152 in Clifton, the township's only two villages. Clifton, which has been lauded for its "grace, quiet, patina of time" but has also been called "the smallest and least interesting little hamlet in Ohio," is in the eastern part of the township and is its oldest town, founded in 1833 by some "enterprising Yankees" in the business of land surveying. A few decades earlier, the site had been chosen for its strategic location along the Little Miami River, a site that surveyors correctly judged would be perfect for a mill. One of these enterprising Yankees was none other than Benjamin Whiteman, the general who petitioned the legislature to keep his property in Greene County.

Whiteman was part of the family who had already settled another town in Ohio called Alpha. Protesting unfavorable land decisions was a pastime that apparently ran in the family, as the family moved wholesale to what would become Clifton when Xenia instead of Alpha was made the county seat. Whiteman was especially annoyed about being skipped over because the house he and his wife lived in was also the county courthouse, the first in the county. (The courthouse mentioned above, where township divisions were hatched, was the courthouse chosen instead of Whiteman's.) Recovering from the slight, Whiteman and his father-in-law built a mill and a tavern in Clifton, donated land for a church, and hired a carpenter to build no less than fourteen houses in the first year, all of which sold. Whiteman would go on to found another town, Ludlow, north of the township.

At its height, Clifton had a number of distilleries, mills, and manufacturers. Their services drew visitors from as far as twenty-five miles away; sometimes these visitors had to wait in lines of thirty or more wagons to unload their grain. However, the stagnant water of the mill's dam "infected the air with ague," killing a number of residents and inducing many to move to healthier locales.

In 1849 Clifton was ravaged by the "worst Cholera epidemic for any town in Ohio based on its size," losing half of its residents in the process. The epidemic started in the tavern when an unknown man died overnight. Nine more people in the tavern and the dwelling next door were stricken before the disease spread through the village. Wastewater was likely the cause of the outbreak: wastewater, when dumped onto porous limestone, traveled through the rock and settled in wells, where it "render[ed] not only possible, but, in many cases, necessary, the defilement of drinking water with products of disease." The tavern and the dwelling used the same well.

Clifton weathered the cholera storm but never regained the numbers of its pre-illness population. An impressive opera house was built in 1943 and is still in operation, with seating for more than three times Clifton's population. The historic Clifton Mill is a draw during today's holiday season, when its impressive, still-working grist mill is covered by more than four million Christmas lights. An eight-person crew begins putting up the display in September; it takes until March to take it down and put it away. December's electric bill runs into the "tens of thousands of dollars."

Despite the geologic underpinning that facilitated cholera outbreaks, the area is profoundly beautiful. The two branches of the Yellow Springs Creek cut their way through stone, as if guided "by the touch of an artist rather than the hammer of Thor." Soft layers of stone have washed away to create the Cascades, a waterfall in what is now the township's Glen Helen Nature Preserve. Tradition holds that this was the Shawnee lovers' preferred trysting place, and this tradition has endured for lovers of today. "Many are the pale face boys and girls who have since known that this trail retains the lure of its Indian tradition," said historian William Albert Galloway. In fact, Susan Smith, the glen's sole ranger, constantly finds people engaged in sexual activity in the preserve, often with little attempt to hide themselves. While most people are apologetic and embarrassed when caught, some lovers get confrontational and refuse to stop when asked. The Cascades are also a favorite spot for summer swimming, which, while a less lubricious pastime, is nonetheless prohibited.

Yellow Springs, located in west Miami Township, took the torch from Clifton to become the township's biggest city. A railroad line fatefully chose the former instead of the latter as a new stop on the line from Cincinnati to Springfield. (While the loss of the railway was "Clifton's Waterloo," the old railway station in Yellow Springs is now remembered by a public bathroom/brochure outlet that looks like a train station.) Many people traveled to Yellow Springs to visit the curative springs, and with the advent of the train station, the town was able to increase its activities as a health resort. Developers began building along a street adjacent to the railroad line and even paid for a church to move so that the strip could be populated with only businesses. Hotels sprung up to cater to the 5,000 people who would sometimes visit the town at the same time.[11] Yellow Springs was officially incorporated in 1856 and by 1908 was a "modern up to date town with over four miles of cement sidewalks" and two telephone systems.

Yellow Springs was briefly the headquarters of the American Hominy Flake Company, which made a product called "Snow

---

11. An 1823 advertisement in the *Columbus Gazette* (published 1817–25) said the springs are "recommended to persons afflicted with bilious affections, chronic constipation, scrofula, dyspepsia, rheumatism and many other diseases. The waters are palatable, cold, clear and sparkling, containing considerable fixed air, and found to be replete with chrystaline [*sic*] particles which, upon being exposed to the action of the air, rust and sink and become bright yellow." An advertisement in the same newspaper a month later said that guests coming to the Yellow Springs Hotel to visit the springs were in no danger of contracting "milk sickness," a fever that afflicted cattle after they consumed *Eupatorium ageratoides* (white snake root) or *Rhus toxicodendrum* (poison ivy), toxic plants common to the area. The fever gave cattle "the trembles" before it killed them. Humans were susceptible to the illness upon drinking the milk of afflicted cows, and this is how Horace Mann, renowned president of Antioch College and "victor for humanity," died in 1843.

Flake," a healthful product that may be "the world's first prepared breakfast cereal." The product was introduced at Philadelphia's National Food Exhibition in 1890, its arrival heralded by the company's founder playing a trombone. The company produced almost three million pounds of the product before it took a turn for the unsuccessful, a downfall initiated by a lawsuit alleging that the company had stolen the patent from a man in nearby Springfield. The case was ruled in favor of the latter man. He was not an adept cereal producer and had "considerable trouble in getting ahold of the [new] machinery" necessary to keep the company producing on par with demand. Stalled, the company closed for good and the factory was dismantled.

CHAPTER 2

The Debate about Breakfast's Legality Resurfaces

Section 4 of the Miami Township Board of Trustees agenda for September 9 was a partial list of the correspondence and email the trustees had received since the last meeting. There were dispatches from the Ohio Department of Transportation, information about the trustees' HMOs, and an announcement of a Greene County Association township dinner. The township had also received the current issue of the *Ohio Township News* magazine, a bimonthly publication from the Ohio Township Association (OTA) that features articles such as "What Does It Take to Educate Residents through a Newsletter?" It had also received the OTA's monthly newsletter, "Grassroots Clippings," a smaller and timelier version of its sister publication. It was customary to go over the received correspondence at the meeting, so Mucher read aloud a few choice pieces of mail.

In addition, the township had received a missive from the Greene County Combined Health District. While the letter to the township didn't specifically address the bed-and-breakfast controversy, rogue B&Bs were a hot-button issue in Miami Township and had recently brought Greene County Combined Health District (GCCHD) officials to the township on numerous occasions. Had Spracklen been at the September 9 meeting, he might have shuddered or clenched his teeth at the very mention of that cursed entity, for, as mentioned, Spracklen was effectively an Erik

Owen himself, appealing the GCCHD's decision to drop the hammer on the Yellow Springs Country Bed and Breakfast, the one he owned. It was a situation that had yet another level of intrigue: the township itself owned a B&B, the Grinnell Mill (located literally around the corner from the Glen House Inn.

But it wasn't just Owen and Spracklen who were being checked out by the GCCHD. The county was doing an investigation of more than a dozen township B&Bs to ensure that they were compliant with Ohio Code. (It was in this dragnet that the problem with the Glen House Inn's septic system was uncovered.) Almost all the B&Bs investigated were able to remain in operation with no problem, but the Glen House Inn and Country B&B proved to have significant issues that needed to be addressed.

In fact, it was Spracklen's inn that kicked off the investigation in the first place, when a family threatened to sue him after being exposed to bats. In the course of looking into the bats, the GCCHD uncovered the existence of "community breakfasts" taking place at the Country B&B every Tuesday, in which up to sixty guests partook in lavish spreads of food and conversation. Spracklen's inn did not have the proper certifications to serve food in this amount, and the violation was compounded by the fact that the woman organizing and cooking the breakfasts had previously been shut down at least twice for doing the same thing out of her home in Yellow Springs. So began another tussle between a B&B and the GCCHD. The township's idealistic resolve exemplified almost two centuries ago by such groups as the Owenite community apparently continues today with the principled stands of area B&B owners and that most incendiary of meals, breakfast.

Trustee Lamar Spracklen is a farmer, and his family has been farming in Miami Township for generations. One can see it in his physical bearing—a few of the tips of his fingers permanently bend at unconventional angles, and he walks with a slight limp that bespeaks a lifetime of strenuous physical labor. Spracklen can trace his ancestors back to the Fergusons, who came to Clifton in the 1830s by way of the Carolinas. Opposed to slavery, they left the South, bought farmland in the area, and took up what would become the family profession. Spracklen's paternal grandfather and family came to Clifton in the 1900s, also to work on a farm; Spracklen's parents were farmers too, though they worked someone else's land. Spracklen is the first in his family to own his

FIGURE 9. Trustee Lamar Spracklen. Photo courtesy of the *Yellow Springs News*.

own farmland, and the tradition continues with Spracklen's sons, who are also area farmers. Typical for Ohio, they grow corn and soybeans and raise cattle. Spracklen's homestead is on a sprawling property on the western edge of the township, though he and his sons own a number of noncontiguous properties on which they farm. Spracklen's daughter lives on a property next door to his own, and she is a high school English teacher in nearby Cedarville.

As far as Spracklen can recall, he is the only trustee who has ever been a farmer, and, as such, much of his perspective as a trustee concerns the livelihood of farmers. Come Election Day, he usually sweeps up votes in the county but doesn't tend to win those in the city. Nevertheless, he was a trustee from 1999 until he retired in 2014 and was replaced by a man named John Eastman.[12] Eastman had run for a number of state and local offices over the

---

12. One person, said Spracklen quit being a trustee because, when coupled with the income from his farm and his retirement, the position made his taxes too complicated.

years, but his desire for political appointment was never gratified until he won a seat as township trustee in the 2013 elections. (A shed on his brother's property is partly sided with various "Eastman for Office" election signs.) However, Eastman tragically died of a heart attack a year into office at age sixty-seven, and Spracklen was selected by the other trustees to complete his term.

Spracklen himself got his start in political office when he was asked to be on the township's Zoning Commission. He served on this commission while also on the Greene County Soil Conservation Board for eighteen years, at one point becoming the director of the Ohio Soil Conservation District. After eighteen years' worth of monthly meetings, Spracklen decided he'd had enough, but then he was asked to run for trustee. Considering that his livelihood came from farming (and still does), he was particularly interested in zoning and the way taxes were spent, as farmland is valued higher and therefore farmers pay higher taxes on the land they own. (An acre of farmland in Miami Township currently costs around $8,000. "You buy it retail and sell it wholesale," Spracklen said.) Thus he ran for trustee in 1999, winning his first term, and, excluding the brief interlude when Eastman was trustee, he has been a trustee ever since. He was finishing out this term during the two contentious meetings of September 2015, and, along with Mucher's, his seat was up for grabs in the elections that were to take place in November of that year.

In 2004, Spracklen bought the property on which his bed-and-breakfast sits, with the old stone farmhouse (built 1828) still intact. "Normally farmhouses are a liability," Spracklen said, but due to its quality build, he didn't need to undertake any serious rehabilitation. He restored it a bit, removing lead paint and putting in new wiring, and in 2006 applied for a variance that said he could run a bed-and-breakfast without having to live there. The variance was granted and the Country Bed and Breakfast opened for business in June 2006.

Operations ran smoothly until undue attention was brought to the B&B in 2015. A family of six staying at the B&B over the July 4th weekend reported bats in their rooms. Spracklen went to the B&B and captured three bats, which were set free. The family alerted local authorities about a possible rabies incident, and it was suggested that they consult with a physician when they arrived home from vacation. The doctor recommended they undergo a rabies vaccination, as they had slept in a room with bats that of course had not been tested for rabies. Exposure to rabies requires a series of four notoriously painful shots given in the upper arm (and an additional shot given when the first one is administered). The family considered suing Spracklen for the cost of the treatment (which they said was $7,000) and the emotional duress of getting the shots.

The bat problem was compounded by the presence of one Norah Byrnes, a Yellow Springs resident who ran a community breakfast operation from Spracklen's kitchen in his B&B. As mentioned in Chapter 1, B&Bs are allowed to serve breakfasts provided they are not served to more people than the number of guests in the establishment. The community breakfasts at the Country Bed and Breakfast were substantially larger: more than sixty people were at the breakfasts each week, with guests able to put in custom orders for food or partake in the lavish buffet of quiche, cereal, pastries, and meats, with coffee poured by people walking around with carafes refilling cups. Norah did most of the cooking, but friends volunteered as waitstaff and prep cooks. Guests sat family-style at tables with multiple seats, an arrangement said to engender a uniquely communal environment. Everyone was welcome and there was no charge to eat, though donations were tacitly accepted via a pitcher located somewhere in the dining room. To attendees, it was a big communal meal; to dispassionate officials, it looked like a bustling restaurant.

Unlike the Glen House Inn controversy, nobody had complained about Norah's breakfast, and in fact the occasion had widespread community support. But the scope of the operation stunned the GCCHD. As in the case of the Glen House Inn, the GCCHD demanded that the Country Bed and Breakfast immediately cease serving the large breakfast and said the B&B would be able to serve food on such a scale only if the appropriate updates to the building and kitchen were done. And, like Owen, Spracklen deemed the cost of the updates prohibitive and the demands unreasonable. The fate of the community breakfasts was in limbo as Spracklen decided what to do.

Norah Byrnes wears the pulled-back hair of a harried cook and a serious expression that makes her appear that she is always scrutinizing something. She grew up in Yellow Springs and is one of three sisters who live in town, all three of whom are said to be "forces of nature." She has loved to cook her entire life and is renowned for her impressive culinary skills. She had been the cook at a Yellow Springs coffee shop, where she developed the well-regarded breakfast menu before she began serving breakfasts from her home in the middle of Yellow Springs in early 2011.

The breakfasts began rather by accident. Byrnes lived adjacent to the parking lot that held the weekend farmers market in Yellow Springs, and her husband would set up a little table in the front yard and sell produce. As he would sit out there all morning, Byrnes would make him breakfast. Passersby would see the delicious plate in front of him and ask if they could have some too. Pretty soon she began inviting people inside.

As more people came to her house to eat, the scope of the meal evolved. The idea was to serve a free breakfast to anyone who wanted it, with payment made through donation but certainly not expected. For her, food was a unifier and a way to open each other up to humanity's best sides, and people seemed to truly appreciate this approach.

"I would like to demonstrate what can happen if you trust everyone and you include everyone," she said. "People are transformed when they sit down and eat together. It's not just about food but fellowship."

Many friends, neighbors, and community members shared her sentiment and came to her house to eat, as did travelers and strangers who had heard about the meals through-word of-mouth. It just grew, and grew very fast, she said. She did no advertising, had no Twitter account—"people just voted with their feet." Soon Byrnes was serving breakfast multiple days per week to a few dozen people each time. And soon a complaint was made to the GCCHD regarding "unsafe food handling practices," while another complainant expressed concern that the size of the breakfasts violated neighborhood zoning laws. Her home was in a residentially zoned area, which allowed for, but limited the scope of, home-based businesses. According to Ohio Code, up to 115 meals can be served per week without any food-safety licensure. Officials found that she was serving fewer than the allowable number of meals and asked her to post a sign in her house effectively saying that guests were eating at their own risk.

However, village code supersedes Ohio Code, which meant that she could serve up to forty meals per week *only if* her operation fell under the parameters of a home-based business. According to village code, no more than 20 percent of a home's square footage may be used for commercial purposes, and client visits are limited to eight per day. The issue came down to whether her breakfasts constituted a home business or not. The fact that no money was requested for the service (but did technically change hands) made the classification unclear.

Village officials ruled that because her home was zoned residential, the activities would have to stop. Byrnes and her supporters were deflated but not defeated. The easiest way to get the Byrnes breakfasts back on their feet was to petition to have her house rezoned to be in the Commercial Business District, a commercially zoned area whose border was the street in front of the house. Theoretically this would make rezoning easier, as the boundary could do a quick jog up and around Byrnes's house, bringing it into the fold, not unlike the way Benjamin Whiteman got boundaries rewritten to bring him back into Greene County. One official commented that Yellow Springs had many spot-zoned establishments, owing to the ubiquity of home-based businesses in the town. (There are many massage therapists, Reiki healers, and similar such enterprises in Yellow Springs.) As it happened, the village was in the process of revising its zoning ordinances, making it an auspicious time to broach the subject. A special zoning meeting was convened a few months later.

But at the meeting, observers and breakfast fans were surprised to see that the idea of rezoning her house was not well received. Residents who weren't as keen on the breakfasts argued that the traffic increase associated with the breakfasts made parking difficult for neighbors and disrupted the tranquility of an otherwise peaceful neighborhood. Their concerns weren't unfounded: the breakfasts became so popular that a semitruck would deliver pallets' worth of food to Byrnes's home. The plan was sunk, Byrnes lay low, and area residents had to make their own breakfasts. In one interview, Byrnes said that "the story is not about [her]—it is about what the community wants and needs," and she declined to comment further.

This is where Spracklen and the Country Bed and Breakfast stepped in, as Spracklen offered the Yellow Springs Country

B&B to Byrnes as a place where she could resume the community breakfasts. The community was overjoyed and flocked there to eat; cars parked up and down the country road in front of the B&B once a week. However, after about a year of breakfasts, Byrnes was once again shut down. The GCCHD said it was less an issue of what constitutes a home businesses and more so one about the safe handling of food: even if the service is donation-only, an establishment or a person still needed a license to serve perishable food.

Deb Leopold, the Director of Environmental Health Services at the GCCHD, said the crackdown had nothing to do with Byrnes's prior run-ins with county authorities. Despite this assurance, some residents were outraged at the forced closure of the hallowed tradition.

"When someone put the care and love into preparing food like that, you can taste it. [Byrnes] has the capacity to bring the community together over food, and that's amazing," said Yellow Springs resident Sandy King. "I want to know who would complain about what she's doing. What—we can't love each other a few hours a week without the authorities coming down on us?"

But the entreaties fell on deaf ears: Spracklen would have to significantly upgrade his facilities if he wanted to serve food in such an amount. (Leopold said that she gave the establishment a few options for continuing the breakfasts, including applying for temporary five-day food-service exemptions up to ten times per year, but Spracklen refused these concessions. Such exemptions are usually granted to one-time events featuring food wagons, for things like festivals and community events.)

One may argue that the rules are there for a reason and that the GCCHD's rules are there to protect the public from unsafe buildings and food-service practices. But equally intense is the desire for people to share the comforts of home, whether by having a party at a commodious B&B or by serving a free, gourmet breakfast to anyone who wants it. Though the latter is not codified by law, it is enshrined in the law of human decency. Spracklen and Byrnes decided to appeal to the notion of human decency, and each made his case to the authorities in the fall of 2015.

Spracklen took his case to the October 2015 meeting of the GCCHD Board of Trustees meeting. The meeting took place in at the Health Department building in Xenia, in a room with dark-colored walls, fancy swivel chairs, and essentially modern projectors—a venue with a feel different from the more low-key multipurpose room of the Miami Township Fire and Rescue building. The B&B issue was the first topic to be addressed. The trustees called on Spracklen to make his case. He stood and began talking. They cut him off and asked him to address the meeting from the podium at the head of the table. Spracklen asked if they were serious, and they said yes. He rolled his eyes and lumbered toward the front of the room, weaving around the officials and community members sitting around the table.

"I'm an individual. I own a bed-and-breakfast. Now I'm told I have to shut it down," Spracklen began. From an objective standpoint, standing at the podium did seem a little more professional and thus added a bit more gravitas to his case. Spracklen gave a history of how he came to run the B&B and how Byrnes came to work there. He said he was told that providing free meals to people was against the law and that if he continued he would be fined $100 per meal and be prosecuted. He repeated this last threat twice, emphasizing the indignity of it all. He also spoke in his capacity as a township trustee, imploring the officials to consider the economic effects the closure would have on the community. He made his case and ended with a vague threat.

"Township trustees are now involved, so just remember, the county's prosecutor is our prosecutor too," he said.

Dan Rudolf, the township's premier citizen-defender of B&Bs, spoke to the board and made the same case that he did for the Glen House Inn. A few other concerned citizens and fellow B&B proprietors spoke in Spracklen's defense. Spracklen also intimated that the bat issue that led to investigation in the first place wasn't entirely his fault. According to a letter sent to him by the family outlining their intentions to sue, they said they left their kids unattended in a room, upon which the kids opened the chimney flue and let the bats in, one of which alighted on a lampshade. Spracklen said he offered to kill the bats, but the Health Department said he couldn't because they were an endangered species.

Officials said the notion that they were unwilling to work with B&B operators was a "gross mischaracterization." Moreover, they weren't in the business of conducting "witch hunts" and had investigated only because of citizen complaints. In fact, the investigation wouldn't ever have even happened had it not been for the objections of concerned residents. The debate unfolded much like that surrounding the Glen House Inn: owner occupancy and zoning code were the primary points of contention.

Once again, the GCCHD officials had to judge with detachment. Deb Leopold said she was glad the community presented such a perfervid take on the issue, but community acclaim does not exempt an establishment from the law. The breakfasts were not allowed to continue because they were simply too far outside the limits of even a creative interpretation of code. Spracklen scowled at the room and sat back down, his mind abuzz with his next move. (A 2015 year-in-review newsletter issued by the GCCHD featured a full page dedicated to the area's B&B controversies.)

Byrnes was going on her fourth month without a venue to serve her breakfasts when this ruling was made. To someone like Byrnes, who viewed her cooking as an act of love and a form of community service, the moratorium was stifling to her very existence. With the Country Bed and Breakfast no longer a viable option, Byrnes appeared before the Yellow Springs Planning Commission in November 2015 to lay out her plans to resume serving breakfasts in her own home. The village council chambers were packed with at least forty supporters, at least ten of whom testified—some in tears—about how wonderful and meaningful her breakfasts were.

While nobody in the room truly wanted to see the breakfasts stopped, they couldn't just let someone run what was essentially a restaurant out of her home—it had to look like a large party, and nothing more. And so code was creatively interpreted in such a way that she could resume breakfasts at her home, but in a reduced capacity. After looking at some diagrams of the layout of Byrnes's home, the BZA ruled that the percentage of her home used for restaurant purposes was within the limit established by law, not because it only took up the allowable 20 percent of the home's space—it didn't, as people ate breakfast all over the house—but because the space was used only 20 percent of the week. They also determined that she could accommodate forty clients per week, slightly bending the rule of eight people per day.

"You're not going to have GFS semitrucks delivering to your house this time, are you?" asked one BZA member.

"No," Byrnes said.

The ruling was a victory, but not quite to the degree that Byrnes and her supporters wanted. Deb Leopold, who was quietly hissed by villagers when she stood up to speak, said that reopening Byrnes's home to breakfasters hinged on making sure the appropriate fire and safety codes were met, a stipulation that may have necessitated visits from bodies that made these respective determinations. Moreover, because the village code's forty-guest limit superseded Ohio Code's 115-meal limit, Byrnes would have to petition the village council to revise village bylaws. One council member cautioned that based on the council's schedule, such a change may take up to two years. There was still work to be done, but breakfast was still on the table. "In the meantime, however," said one newspaper at the time, "after she meets the county requirements, her breakfasts can resume, in a reduced but nonetheless deliciously legal capacity."

Considering the recent tumult over the operations of area bed-and-breakfasts, thinly veiled accusations were often lobbed at the trustees by people on both sides of the B&B dispute about their questionable impartiality, as the Miami Township Board of Trustees ran the Grinnell Mill Bed & Breakfast, which is less than a mile away from the Glen House Inn. Naturally, one side accused the trustees of ruling against the Glen House in order to prop up the business of the Grinnell Mill, while the other side said that the trustees were prejudiced against the wishes of the non-B&B-owning neighbors. According to the trustees, running the B&B wasn't a moneymaking scheme but rather a "monument to the long milling history of the Little Miami River," a place where guests could enjoy the tranquility of their surroundings while getting a sense of the long history of the township.

The original mill was built on the site in 1813, though, as was often the case with buildings at the time, it burned down and had to be rebuilt in 1821. A man named Frank Grinnell bought the mill in 1864, lending his name not only to the mill but to many streets, neighborhoods, and landmarks in the area. The dam that fed the mill was upstream from the Little Miami River and was 100 feet long. Water from the dam powered the waterwheel, thanks to a 1,000-foot millrace. The amount of water needed to power the mill was carefully calibrated, because much of the water was diverted back to the river before it entered the mill. After decades of gristmill service (including the addition of a saw-mill and a limestone-processing facility), the mill closed in 1937 due to illness in the area and a lack of business. Antioch College acquired the property when they expanded the Glen Helen Nature Preserve in 1948, but the college wasn't sure what to do with the old mill, and it grew increasingly dilapidated as time went by.

The Miami Township Trustees, in the interest of maintaining the historic building, decided to intercede. They decided to open a bed-and-breakfast in the mill building, as the building had a few rooms that would be perfect for guests. In the calming environs of the surrounding woods, one could (and still can) explore the foundation of the millrace and an old family cemetery. In 2004, the township partnered with Glen Helen and the Yellow Springs Historical Society to create a nonprofit organization that would reopen the mill and run it as a B&B, which Mucher said was "negotiated out of Antioch's hands." The township doesn't own the land that the mill is on but rather is leasing it for 100 years.

Some fellow area history buffs got involved in restoring the building, which included significant structural and roofing work and then spiffy new coats of paint. One area man named Jim Hammond got involved with the project, as he said he had a "weakness for restoring historic artifacts."[13] (Previous projects included restorations of a carousel, an airplane, and a fire engine.) Hammond put much of his own money into restoring the building and even rebuilt part of the paddle wheel based solely on old photographs. Others volunteered to clean and cook or to host the mill's open hours, which initially were four hours every day, starting when the Grinnell Mill Bed & Breakfast opened for business in 2008.

The idea of having a B&B there was to maintain the building and keep it from being torn down, said Richard Zopf, who helped get the Grinnell Mill B&B project up and running. As such, it wasn't characterized as an aggressive business model but rather made just enough money to keep it going. With only two rooms to let, the B&B wasn't likely to generate significant revenue, and

---

13. The Hammond family is also the brainchild behind the Mills Park Hotel, a twenty-eight-room Southern Revival hotel in downtown Yellow Springs; its construction from 2014 to 2016 was (literally) the biggest thing to happen to the village in years.

the township originally set aside money from its own budget to pay the expenses, including those of a caretaker who lived on-site. This "didn't work out that well in practice," said Mucher, and the operations were amended so that the township wasn't footing so much of the bill.

But the trustees found themselves in a bit of a pickle when the mill proved to make enough money that it couldn't be considered a nonprofit. The trustees were advised to undertake a complex bookkeeping arrangement, in which the nonprofit that ran the mill started a separate corporation that can make money which it can in turn donate to the mill. Nevertheless, Mucher said the township didn't make any money from the mill and maintained the B&B "simply in the interest in preserving an old building."

Unlike the neighboring Glen House Inn, the township's B&B has not been rocked with scandal or complaints (although the trustees did have to evict the previous innkeeper over a dispute about who should pay the property taxes on the building. The innkeeper then went to work for . . . the Glen House Inn(!), where she prepared for visitors "the homemade granola she made famous at the Grinnell Mill"). Perhaps neighbors had a little more confidence in the operations of a facility created and overseen by the trustees, as they can rest assured that all strictures and official codes are being followed. While the mill is open to school groups and business meetings, such bookings aren't frequent enough to feel like a "rogue bed-and-breakfast [that was] disturbing the peace of an otherwise quiet neighborhood." And even the most punctilious scrutinizers of area B&B activity can take comfort in knowing that the trustees are serving only the amount of food such a business is allotted, and not a muffin or eggs Benedict more.

Update: Spracklen continues to run the bed-and-breakfast, but without the lavish breakfasts supplied by Byrnes. He has "no use for the Health Department," and he doesn't care who knows it, he said, adding that he has heard from many people that the GCCHD is the "most unreasonable health department in Ohio." Beyond that, he was done with the issue and wasn't interested in talking about it in any more depth. The bed-and-breakfast is currently up for sale, as Spracklen said he is getting tired of paying the bills, but he also isn't hell-bent on selling it and isn't making a truly concerted effort to unload it. As for his stint as a trustee, he plans to continue serving as a trustee as long as he can in order to see a few projects through to completion. Despite the ruling in her favor, Byrnes did not resume serving breakfast from her home. She currently cooks for a few area businesses and is considering what to do next. The township continues to run the Grinnell Mill Bed & Breakfast, accommodating the occasional guest or event, but keeps its festivities within reason.

CHAPTER 3

"A Quarter-Inch of Chaos"

At the 2015 APWA Southwestern Ohio
Snow and Ice Removal Conference

Continuing on with item (2) on the September 9 agenda, the examination of the recent correspondence, Mucher mentioned the township's insurance policies and a back-and-forth email exchange to set up a bike-route designation meeting. (Miami Township has dozens miles of rail trails, part of a network of hundreds of mile of bike trails made from old railroads, one of the best such trail systems in the country.) But one of the most interesting bits of correspondence was the penultimate item on the list: an email confirming the township's registration for the 2015 APWA Southwestern Ohio Snow and Ice Removal Conference, a biannual affair designed to help local governments manage the inevitable hazards of winter. "Put on your best snow boots," Mucher said.

The 2015 conference, hosted by the American Public Works Association fifty miles away at the Sharonville Conference Center, featured speakers from road departments from all around the state. Attendees could behold a dozen shiny new snowplow trucks in the showroom and commingle with a number of other vendors plying relevant trades, such as custom municipal sign making and pipe repair, the latter offered by a company that applied a proprietary sealant to the inside of broken pipes. (Their slogan was "We only do what the pipe tells us it needs.") The keynote speaker of the conference was Diana Clonch, a thirty-year public-works veteran who is now a successful freelance winterization consultant.

FIGURE 10. Shiny, brand-new plows on display at 2015 APWA Southwestern Ohio Snow and Ice Removal Conference. Photo by Dylan Taylor-Lehman.

It was Mucher who typically made the trip to the conference, and Gochenouer, the cemetery sexton and a road crewman (he is now the head of the road department), usually went with him. Neither Gochenouer nor Mucher was particularly excited about attending. It wasn't that the conference was totally boring, Gochenouer said, but that it wasn't especially helpful. Attendees had to sit through a few hours of presentations to get a few minutes' worth of usable information. The presentations usually consisted of experts from around the state talking about how they solved a problem or adapted equipment to the needs of their jurisdiction. While Gochenouer could appreciate their ingenuity from a professional standpoint, the lessons didn't always apply to the needs of Miami Township. A speaker from Franklin County (which includes Ohio's capital, Columbus) discussed strategies needed to deal with its 770 miles of roads: around two million gallons of antiwinter liquids annually and the use of semitrucks to spray the liquids onto the roads. Miami Township, on the other hand, has less than fourteen miles of roads and three trucks, a fleet occasionally augmented by the plows that residents attached to their personal vehicles.

"Any questions, Mark?" Mucher asked after announcing the conference.

"Nope," Crockett said.

The other officials quietly avoided comment when registration was confirmed, lest they be roped into going.

The first official road in Miami Township was laid out on March 3, 1822. There were several "so-called roads" before then, but they were "scarcely traversable." Michael A. Broadstone wrote that roads improved year by year and most were "at least graveled" by the time he penned his *History of Greene County, Ohio* in 1918. By 2015, the township had exactly 13.43 miles of roads, almost all of them paved.

Road maintenance is within the purview of the trustees, a duty that includes everything from filling potholes to maintaining culverts to implementing full-scale winterization efforts. The township fleet is three trucks (two of which have dumping capabilities), one twenty-six-year-old panel van, and a phalanx of tractors and lawnmowers. Each spring the township develops a road budget based on the work anticipated for the year, prioritizing repairs on the worst roads and any new equipment that needs to be purchased. Road maintenance is an ongoing project, and one that occasionally requires outside help. Sometimes neighboring Bath Township, which has a paving machine, will do a little work in Miami Township in trade for future help with its needs. Miami Township works with neighboring municipalities to make what is called a "collective bid" for their collective asphalting or resurfacing needs. Participating jurisdictions add up what needs to be done—a half-mile stretch here, a hundred square yards there—and submit a report to the county, which contracts all the work to one company as one job. Doing it this way allows municipalities to save money, as everyone getting work done at the same time splits the cost of mixing asphalt and dispatching trucks and police. Once in awhile, the county will determine that part of a road now lies in Miami Township, which may add to their mileage-based clout but also means that the township is responsible for maintaining that much more road.

Miami Township has the dubious distinction of hosting the first vehicular accident in Greene County. Lodrick Austin, a stagecoach driver, was killed when his coach overturned on September 1, 1836. He lost control coming down a hill on Clifton Road, was thrown from the vehicle, and struck a large rock. Austin is buried in Clifton Cemetery, and his tombstone features an ornate horse and a coach, which perhaps seems a little insulting to the deceased's memory.[14] The accident occurred no more than 200 feet from where Austin ended up being buried, and the carving appears to reference the very tragedy that befell him: a female passenger sits in the carriage but the carriage has no driver, just as the accident had happened on that fateful September day.

Vehicular accidents are of course a fact of life in Miami Township, and, like everywhere else in the United States, they happen with greater frequency in the winter. Snow and ice are indiscriminate perils, and all it takes is a small amount of snow, "a quarter-inch of chaos," said one township official, to throw a city into bedlam.

As little as a quarter-inch of snow means erratic drivers, slick roads, and breaking asphalt as water freezes and expands. It means more accidents, more calls for the Miami Township Fire and Rescue, and a significant amount of preparation for the township. Potholes need to be filled, salt has to be stockpiled, and the township's trucks, with their spreaders and dump buckets, almost certainly require maintenance. (All bridges in any jurisdiction are the county's responsibility.)

While it was Mucher and Gochenouer who ended up attending the Snow and Ice Removal Conference again, the event at least offered them a day out of town and the chance to pick up some new winterization life hacks. Thinking of the good they might be able to do for the township, they met at the township's fleet garage to leave for the conference at 7:00 a.m. Both were early.

They weren't driving one of the township's work trucks but Mucher's golden Chrysler minivan, "The Muchmobile," as Gochenouer called it. Mucher said his van was frequently the de facto work vehicle, as most of the township's vehicles had only two seats. The Muchmobile crunched on the gravel and wound its way through the township to the highway.

---

14. *Echoes,* a publication of the Ohio Historical Society featured a front-page article about the headstone in its October 1962 issue. The author of the article said he found the Lodrick Austin headstone by accident when he went to look for the grave of a person whose coffin was said to be making strange sounds when it was buried. The sounds were so eerie that the funeral party decided to proceed with the burial instead of investigating what the sounds could be. They wanted to leave the site as soon as possible.

Mucher didn't have much experience in winterizing cities when he became a trustee in 1996. He had operated a video rental and film development business in Yellow Springs for more than twenty years, before digital film and video streaming proved the "ultimate fatality" for his career. When he was still in business, he struck up a friendship with Wilbur Deaton, the man who ran the hardware store across the street and who had worked as the township clerk and then its zoning inspector. They had coffee every morning and developed a mentor-mentee type of friendship. Mucher was interested in becoming more involved in the community, and Deaton encouraged him to apply for a recently vacated trustee seat. So Mucher submitted an application, had a few interviews, and was offered the job. It proved to be just what he was looking for, a "low impact political job" that carried a lot of responsibility but one that still left him time to run his own business and spend time with his wife and three kids. Once in office, he read "every page of meeting minutes since 1934," attended conventions and seminars, and read the Ohio Revised Code front to back. He has been reelected in every election since then. He is able to talk about winterization both fluently yet dispassionately, the hallmark of an experienced professional. "We plow the roads and put down salt, bury people, put out their fires—you can't get a whole lot more grassroots than that," he said.

Being able to have his fingers in so many pies fits with his disposition as well. "I like micromanaging," he said. "I tend to be a bit overbearing in township administration. I wish I could be a little more laid back. I'm sure if you ask anybody, they'll say I stick my nose into everything." But it's also that kind of ethic that truly serves to get the work done, and Mucher cited the maxim that it's easier to ask for forgiveness than ask for permission.

Gochenouer is also a man who can get things done, but more so on the street or in a ditch than in the MTFR meeting room. He has a perpetually sunburned neck, a moustache, and a Leatherman tool on his belt that he can readily employ in many different ways; he exudes hands-on experience of the kind that only a lifetime of fixing things can foster. Gochenouer's tenure working for the township preceded Mucher's. He was working part-time until a long-time employee retired, allowing him to become the number two road crewman. When that crewman retired, Gochenouer took the top spot.

On the way to Sharonville, the two discussed other trade show conferences they'd been to and whether free lunch was included or not. It wasn't always. Registration for the 2015 Snow and Ice Conference cost $35 per person but at least included lunch. The topic settled, the two lapsed into a short silence. The day was gray and chilly, with a steady rain. The heater hummed and the windshield wipers squeaked.

Conversation picked back up again a few minutes later.

"You working on that dandelion quote?" Mucher asked.

The abundance of dandelions in the township had to be dealt with.

"Some people eat them," Gochenouer said.

True, Mucher said. And some people make wine out of them too. But then both admitted they weren't sure which part of the dandelion was used for the winemaking process.

A little while later, Mucher indicated a passing truck belonging to Jurgensen Asphalt Companies.

"There are your friends," he said.

Gochenouer nodded.

"They're the best," he said, sincerely.

He would know. Gochenouer said he came from an asphalt background. For one, he had spent a lot of time driving on it, he joked. But more seriously, he said, he started working on an asphalt crew right after high school, one of the many labor and construction jobs he's had from an early age. His dad always made sure he was working on different projects and was comfortable around all kinds of machines. The idea was that his skills and experience would ensure he was always employable. "If you're not working, it's because you don't want to," he said.

A truck driving erratically on the highway prompted the mention that he'd also been a truck driver. He'd driven for twelve years, five of which were long-haul and required him to spend up to seven weeks on the road at a time. He lived in his truck, thousands of miles away from his family and home.

"You'd sit in a waiting room and they'd call your number when a shower was ready," he said, recalling old truck stops. "The shower was free but you'd have to rent the towel."

But it wasn't all bad, he said. Sometimes he'd be on a layover for a few days before linking up with a series of deliveries that would take him back toward home. On these furloughs he and his

FIGURE 11. The parking lot at the Sharonville Convention Center. Note the number of work pickups, most of which bore the emblem of a maintenance department. Photo by Dylan Taylor-Lehman.

fellow truckers would go out and explore whatever city they were waiting in. Gochenouer recalled the beauty of California in particular and the fun of sitting behind the "Hollywood" sign while drinking beer. He'd been run out of Beverly Hills once, he said, for not looking the part. A cop came up to him and asked him what he was doing. "I said I was just looking," Gochenouer recalled, "and the cop said, 'Well, you looked yet?'"

Forty minutes later, the Muchmobile pulled into the conference center parking lot. It was the lone minivan among rows of work trucks with maintenance department insignias. Inside the conference center were the truck drivers, approximately three hundred men with closely cropped hair and goatees. Cell phones were universally clipped to belts, and neon T-shirts were worn in numbers rivaled only by those at an actual construction site. Sixty-five municipalities were represented at the conference, making it "pretty sizable for a local AWPA conference," according to one organizer.

The conference was only one day long. The morning was divided into four 45-minute sessions. One session was earmarked for attendees to check out the showroom, but the other three were presentations. Attendees were divided into four groups that rotated through the sessions. Mucher and Gochenouer were in group (2), meaning that they went to the showroom first.

The conference organizers set out donuts and coffee. Both men took a donut and looked at the trucks, which were shiny and gigantic but ultimately outside the needs of Miami Township. The township's road budget for 2015 was approximately $50,000, and one of the middle-grade trucks cost at least twice that.

Mucher and Gochenouer made their rounds of the booths. One company offered their service of quantifying vehicular idle time. A rep said she did a study of one municipality and found that the time its vehicles spent idling cost the city around $50,000 each year. Plow-route optimization would lead to less idling, and she could help jurisdictions figure out how to optimize plow routes. Despite their entreaties, the sales reps were left empty-handed.

The next two hours and fifteen minutes were dedicated to presentations. Mucher and Gochenouer sat in on these sessions, polite but expressionless, casually listening for those few minutes of valuable information. Though a cell phone would occasion- ally go off (one of the ringtones was a very loud duck-quack) and at least one sleeping attendee could be spotted during each dis- cussion, attendees were privy to much information, as a county's snow and ice removal concerns are many:

Plows tend to throw snow onto the front of trucks, obscuring visibility and blocking air intakes, which can lead to overheating. Plow routes are based on continuous right-hand turns, which is why a representative from Centerville maligned the town's many cul-de-sacs. Plow teams are often on-call for grueling twelve-hour shifts, though this is better than working for sixteen hours at a stretch, a schedule that employees "can't really plan their lives around." Sometimes, the ground will be so cold that even after the air temperature rises, rain will freeze shortly after impact. Is salt brine or beet juice more effective? Is chloride-treated sand the best deicer for gravel roads? Are the township's trucks calibrated properly, and are they actually putting out what their gauges say? "One thing we've been wrestling with for years are standard truck [spark] plugs," said a worker from the Ohio Department of Transportation. Everyone in the audience laughed and nodded. "How many of you have replaced mailboxes?" another speaker asked. Almost everyone raised his hand.

As Gochenouer predicted, the discussions didn't offer univer- sal solutions for these problems but presented the clever ways in which winter emergencies were addressed. Auglaize County faced the problem of equipment not mixing rock salt—"grit," as the presenter called it—well enough into brine. There would still be large patches of ice on the road after it was dispersed, so he and his team retrofitted an asphalt hopper to mix it. The upgrade cost Auglaize County about $31,000, but now they mix 40,000 tons of salt brine per year and even rent out their salt-mixing services, charging neighboring counties and agencies $13 per ton. "A fairly standard amount," he said. The speaker also showed pictures of the custom beet-juice tanks his department built for $600 each.

Diana Clonch's roundtable was one of the four sessions, and she'd spent the morning spitballing with employees. She applauded the imagination she'd seen at the conference. "The more we learn, the more we know how to step outside the box," she said. "If you always do what you've always done, you'll always get what you've always got."

Clonch was tall, with long black hair draped over her shoulder in a thick plait, like a military sash. (She is the past president of the board of the Ohio chapter of the American Public Works Association.) She spoke simply but animatedly, like someone used to public speaking. She seemed friendly and successful, the likely demeanor of someone with degrees in civil engineering and business.

"Do not be ashamed to steal your neighbor's ideas," Clonch advised. "We're all working together in the snow and ice community."

Sometimes friendly rivalry between neighboring counties was a good thing, she said. Plowing a road cleanly all the way to the county line awards bragging rights when you can see that the neighboring county hasn't gotten to their side yet. But more seriously, she said, working with other jurisdictions can be very beneficial because collaboration increases efficiency and saves money. After all, at the heart of it, it's all for the benefit of the people who live there.

Clonch's session was the last of the four for group (2). The attendees walked straight into the two long lines of the lunch buffet: hamburgers, baked beans, chicken, and macaroni and cheese. Plates full, they filed back into the showroom and sat around large folding tables. The tables were in turn surrounded by the trucks on display. It was like eating in a garage on the job.

Mucher and Gochenouer sat with a half-dozen guys, exchanging small talk. Not much more could be said. Anything they could say to each other on the topic of snow removal had likely already

FIGURE 12. Eating lunch among the plows. Photo by Dylan Taylor-Lehman.

been covered in one of the earlier sessions or had been part of the pitch rattled off by a sales rep. At this point, the conference was about as exciting as eating lunch in a garage that looked like the garage they spent time in every day. The Miami Township contingent decided to cut out after lunch, skipping Clonch's keynote speech ("Doing the Right Thing at the Right Time") and the recognition of the 2015 Excellence in Snow and Ice Control Award winner. They'd seen enough throughout the years in Miami Township to have a handle on what they had to do in the coming months.

They walked back to the Muchmobile silently, Gochenouer carrying a can of soda. They knew that, should some surprise crisis pop up, each could be counted on to address it with the professionalism that is an evident part of their bearing. Gochenouer was scrappy and smart; Mucher was thorough and direct. They'd been through two meetings' worth of irate neighbors—what was a quarter-inch of snow?

As it turned out, the winter of 2015–16 proved not to be that bad. Mucher said the township used about 25% the amount of salt normally used; they didn't have to pay for outside plow help; and there were no significant vehicle repairs.

The Noteworthy Buildings, Religious Reformers, and Principled Citizens of Miami Township

In addition to building roads and bed-and-breakfasts, Miami Township has been the home of a number of noteworthy buildings over the years, including what Broadstone simply called "A Famous Barn." The barn, built by John Bryan, was apparently the largest in the entire state, measuring 206 feet long, 120 feet wide, and 75 feet tall, later made even bigger by an L-shaped addition that was "itself larger than the average barn." Some even claimed that the barn was the largest in the world, though a barn in Russia supposedly beat it by a foot on each side. Either way, it was big and fancy: in 1908, the book *Greene County 1803–1908* noted that the barn was "equipped with running water and all modern improvements."

The Neff House, a hotel that replaced another hotel which catered to guests visiting the springs, had a comically large porch that wrapped around all the way around it, a distance of 450 feet. The porch extended twenty feet from the house and was three stories tall, with huge columns reaching to the roof. Inside the hotel were 300 rooms and six bowling alleys, and the stable building out back had 125 stalls. Billed as a "Southern House in the Northwest for Southerners," it also had its own fire department, dairy, orchard, and garden. But, as the saying goes, nothing good can last, and the hotel closed in 1882 as "stage coach clientele declined." The building was dismantled ten years later and the lumber sold to area builders.

Another quirky building was the home of a "communistic" group called the Owenites, who built a "long, rambling house" as a communal home for members who settled in Miami Township in the mid-1820s after their original enclave in Indiana collapsed. Ohio was a hotbed of experimental communities at the time, many of which were based around surprisingly radical notions of shared property and communal money. Most of them had a significant religious bent and were more often than not headed by a charismatic leader who considered himself ordained by God. There were the Shakers, an egalitarian Christian group whose name came from their "rather violent group dancing movements," and the Quakers, who were likewise guided by pacifist and democratic principles but were known for a more sober bearing.

The Owenite community was named after a Welshman and Scotch manufacturer named Robert Owen. His lifetime of pondering the smallest details of human existence began at five years of age when he ate a too-hot spoonful of his breakfast and scalded the inside of his stomach, forever making digestion difficult. "This made me attend to the different qualities of food on my changed constitution," he wrote in his memoirs, "and I have always thought that this accident had a great influence in forming my character."

As Owen grew, his capacity for close reflection turned to the social ills of the day. One of his *causes célèbres* was campaigning against allowing children to work in mills. "Those who entered did so without hope of emerging except as blind or maimed or tubercular wreckage," said one historian. Owen soon became an old-time reformer, publishing scads of leaflets and tracts and traveling around England advocating for the "Owen system of education." His idea of economic and social reform revolved around small, self-sufficient communities, which led him to purchase an entire town in Indiana from the outgoing Rappites, another quirky religious community renowned for the quality of their workmanship and looked at with some suspicion for their avowed celibacy. Owen came to America to negotiate the sale of the town.

The Rappites, "plain, quiet, even stupid-appearing people," according to historian R. E. Banta, sold the Indiana town to Owen because they were heading back east to Pennsylvania, where they originated. The town, called "Harmony," featured mills, shops, orchards, and buildings of all sorts on close to 30,000 acres. When Owen arrived in the United States, he advertised his new community widely and noted that he would pay the expenses of anyone who wanted to settle there and would feed them when they arrived. As a result, over one thousand people flocked to the town. Unlike the incredibly industrious Rappites, the Owenites suffered from a lack of leadership, as Owen had made only two trips to the settlement by the time it fell apart in the mid-1820s. Members abandoned in droves, and some made their way east into Ohio, where they established the Owenite community in Miami Township, which featured the long, rambling house mentioned above.

"The facts concerning this strange settlement [in Miami Township] are obscure," Broadstone says, but it is known that the group shared money and that "no man was considered more important than the other." Likewise, everyone lived and cooked in the large structure. Pitching in was an important part of the group's directive, to the point of doing unfamiliar tasks: "Men who seldom or never before labored with their hands devoted themselves to agriculture and the mechanical arts, with a zeal which was at least commendable, though not always according to knowledge." (A former member offered a less generous appraisal: "The most inefficient members pushed to the superintendency . . . and when rejected, would sulk and shirk . . . fences were used for firewood.") Nevertheless, the phalanstery came together. Each family had its own room, and more rooms were added as the settlement grew. The building was eventually 100 feet long and 20 feet wide. But the settlement folded within two years, partly because of the lack of practical skill and partly because a handful of members were trying to appoint themselves leaders of the group. (Or they may have been smote: "They were professed Christians," said one writer, "but I heard them uttering the most horrible oaths.") According to Broadstone, most of the original members of this group left Greene County, but a few of them remained and became "useful citizens of the township." The building fell into disuse and collapsed, though its foundation was intact for at least the next century.

A few families from the erstwhile community moved to nearby Yellow Springs and continued to hold meetings trumpeting their doctrines. One neighbor recalled they were "great propagandists and appeared to delight in arguing and setting forth their doctrines and theories wherever they could find listeners, as at sales, barn raisings, etc." Development of other Owenite communities was attempted throughout Ohio, but the Miami Township community was the only one that got off the ground.

Another set of reformers announced their plans to move to Yellow Springs in the 1850s, and the announcement was met with assurances that they would never be welcome. A man named T. L. Nichols and his wife, Mary S. Gove Nichols, purchased the Water Cure Establishment health resort facility and had plans to turn it into a resort called the Memnonia Institute, which would be governed by their own philosophy of human betterment. This sounded good on the surface, but rumor had it that the Nicholses advocated "free love." The fact that such an openly immodest group would attempt to set up shop in the community "was looked at as a most outrageous thing from the standpoint of the community," with Antioch's president Horace Mann declaring the institute the "superfoetation or diabolism upon polygamy," a nearly incomprehensible though clearly cutting insult. The Nicholites issued a prospectus challenging the community's perception and outlining the health benefits of the area—an agreeable climate, for one, "with an entire freedom from malaria"—and the actual statutes of the Memnonia Institute, which were not nearly as sexy as people thought. The resort served only vegetarian food and was tobacco-free; daily baths were required of its participants, and, far from being a bastion of free love, the institute was actually designed to "free men and women from the domination of sensual appetites and habits, and their injurious consequences, material and spiritual." Anyone unable to curb her or his inherent licentiousness was not judged per se but would be asked not to participate in the institute. Dr. Nichols was invited to plead his case to a committee of citizens, but the committee was not swayed and asked him to leave, which he did.

Despite these moralistic objections, the area has long been a bastion of progressive thought, a noticeable enclave in what is primarily a red area of a red (sometimes purple) state. In addition to the healers who flocked to the springs and the forward-thinking college that sprang up near them, Miami Township has a long history of involvement in the Underground Railroad and is known for the Conway Colony, a settlement of slaves who had escaped and were brought to Yellow Springs the summer of 1862 by Moncure Daniel Conway, an abolitionist preacher. The families he was escorting were actually the people previously enslaved on his family's plantation. The journey was perilous, and Conway wrote in his autobiography that the people making their way to Ohio barely spoke or slept the entire journey. (The exact number of people who arrived has been lost to history, but it was estimated to have been between thirty and sixty individuals.) Once the travelers arrived in the area, they were able to get work as farmers or domestic help. The group flourished and laid the groundwork for future generations—many families in the township today can trace their roots back to the Conway Colony.

An ex-slave named Wheeling Gaunt also settled in the area in the late 1840s. Gaunt was born a slave in Kentucky in 1812 but was able to buy himself out of servitude in 1845 when he was thirty-three. He didn't leave Kentucky right away, instead electing to stay and work so that he could buy the freedom of his family members, including that of his wife. He was able to do so, and he promptly freed his wife again when he realized that in buying her freedom, he had made her technically his property. All the while, he was amassing properties and became quite wealthy. He moved to Miami Township in the late 1860s, where he continued to buy up land. He donated his land and money to his wife and area institutions before he died at age eighty-two. A stipulation of one of his donations was that proceeds from the land go to feed the area's "poor and worthy widows," starting a tradition of delivering packets of sugar and flour to widows, which continues in the present. His funeral service was "packed to suffocation," and Gaunt Park in Yellow Springs still carries his name.

As police chief, Jim McKee was in a tough position during the civil rights era. McKee, himself a descendent of the Conway Colony, was Ohio's first black police chief and served for thirty-four years, from 1959 to 1993.[15] He was tasked with maintaining order in the village in which he had such historic ties. In 1963, he oversaw the police response to a pivotal moment in area civil rights history, when Gegner's Barbershop, located right in the center of Yellow Springs, became the focal point of area demonstrations.

Lewis Gegner, the barbershop's owner, refused to cut the hair of black patrons. As word of his recalcitrance spread, Antioch students and community activists began going into the shop and occupying spaces in the waiting area, requesting that Gegner cut their hair. He would not acquiesce, so demonstrators would wait until a customer got out of the chair to leave and quickly occupy it before another patron could take a seat. The student-occupiers mounted a peaceful sit-in, reading magazines and offering Gegner a light for his cigarette when he needed it.

Concerned for the safety of the students and obliged to intervene when Gegner said he would press charges, police, under McKee's command, removed student protestors from the shop. More people from both sides of the spectrum were drawn to the barbershop, which soon became a tense proving ground. Photos from the time show crowds spilling out into the street, with the jeering faces of local racists providing a harrowing backdrop to the scene. Local police set up a command post in the hardware store across the street from the barbershop. Feeling the intensity, the hardware store's owner commented that "although he feels he might have made some real money selling sledgehammers, [he] chose to close the doors for safety reasons."

One hundred people were eventually arrested in demonstrations against the barbershop. Gegner closed his doors, sold his shop, and moved away. He never faced any charges for his racist haircutting policies, and the Supreme Court ultimately refused to hear the lawsuit brought against him. Gegner won a sort of sick victory when the dust settled, for, as one newspaper put it, "Gegner had never consented to cut a black man's hair when pressured."

---

15. For more on McKee, see http://www.ysnews.com/old/stories/2003/january/012303_mckee.html.

Despite being a location accepting of escaped slaves, despite the changes wrought by the Gegner protests, and despite the fact that well into the middle of the twentieth century Yellow Springs was the only place in the area where black families could buy or build a home, many feel that the legacy of diversity in the area is actually on the decrease. Increasing property values and an increasingly tourism-based economy have made home and business rental costs higher than ever, edging out those in a lower income bracket and forcing businesses to close up shop. An area that once boasted a population that was 30 percent black, including numerous black business owners and village officials, is now increasingly gentrified, with businesses and homes bought up by well-meaning, well-off white people, who have in turn come to occupy positions of prominence in town.

The difficulties inherent in running a religious community and maintaining a diverse population are perhaps reflective of the human tendency to disagree, not unlike the principled squabbles that characterize Yellow Springs in the present day. Yellow Springs is known not only for its residents' strident left-wing optimism but also for its prolonged debates that retard the progress of the very change they wish to see, whether it is resurfacing sidewalks or attempting to make the community more affordable.

One strange incident from the present day encapsulates all the tricky problems mentioned above: the leadership of the local Black Lives Matter movement was co-opted by a small contingent (three people) of vocal communists. According to one member, the communists were known to shout down the objections of people who didn't feel it necessary to include Mao quotes on leaflets advocating for racial justice and managed to insert themselves into leadership positions of the BLM group by dint of will. The communist contingent even began structuring the group with traditional nomenclature, calling its stable of primarily communist literature the "Political Education" wing of Black Lives Matter. Things came to a head when the communist leadership rejected working with a state senator on legislation that would address the frightening realism of toy guns (the handling of which had recently led to the police killing of an innocent black man named John Crawford III in an area Walmart). The reason the communists rejected working with a mainstream politician was that they felt it would legitimize the faulty system that they vowed to overthrow. This squabble alienated many of BLM's founding members and supporters, and membership of the group gradually grew smaller and smaller. The first incarnation of BLM disbanded and was re-formed not long after by a core group of members, but the initial enthusiasm was scuttled by the communist kerfuffle.[16]

---

16. The re-formed BLM group, calling itself "Black Lives Matter Miami Valley," was successful in getting the authorities to reexamine parts of the John Crawford case, in addition to consistently mounting vigils and demonstrations designed to bring attention to the injustice of his death. Activists contended that the 911 caller exaggerated the threat Crawford was alleged to have posed, which led to the fatal response by law enforcement. The officers involved in the shooting were cleared of any wrongdoing, a decision that activists felt was a complete miscarriage of justice. Using an obscure part of Ohio Code, the group filed affidavits with a municipal court, thereby triggering a reexamination by court officials. A municipal judge found that there was cause to suspect that the caller acted maliciously and referred the case to a prosecutor, who ultimately appointed an attorney to look at the case—the same attorney who had previously commented that the 911 caller was just doing his civic duty. The state attorney general opted not to reexamine the case. Undaunted by such setbacks, the group is quite fierce and quite active and continues to rally around the cause of "Justice for John Crawford."

CHAPTER 4

Procedure

Clearly the principled sentiments that had helped forge township history were displayed in the first part of the meeting on September 9. But, like township events far off in the past, the pivotal determinations from earlier in the meeting were consigned to memory as the evening wore on.

On that note, Mucher wrapped up the correspondence portion of the agenda, and the September 9 meeting was able to move forward to the next item with a brisk, businesslike pace. The efficiency is thanks in part to the way township meetings are conducted, as they follow a logical, tried-and-true format familiar to meetings everywhere: an opening preamble, a roll call, the ayes and nays, the firsting and seconding of motions. The township trustees meetings include all of these, a process called *parliamentary procedure.* Following a brief interlude of chitchat, the group effortlessly lapsed into officialese once the meeting got started.

"Can I get a motion to approve the adoption of the minutes from August 17, 2015?" Mucher asked when the meeting began.

"I'll make that motion," said Crockett.

"And I'll second the motion," Mucher said. "Any further discussion regarding that? Hearing that, may we vote please?"

"Crockett?" said Silliman.

"Yes."

"Mucher?"

"Yes."

The whole process, from opening the meeting to adopting minutes to paying of bills (including reading the individual amounts at a speed rivaling that of the guy in the old Micro Machines commercials), took no more than a minute. A similarly efficient process took care of passing resolutions to appropriate bills and transfer $10,000 from the General Fund to the Cemetery Fund. Placing aside the running of an efficient meeting, political office is a serious undertaking. Imagine trying to make the decision about whether to buy insurance for an entire town, or to upgrade the entire township's computer servers (at a cost of $18,000, in April 2004), or how to go about organizing the burial of indigents who die on township land, as townships are required to do by Ohio Code. None of the trustees had a bureaucratic background, so how did they learn to conduct the proceedings with such dispatch, and how did they learn to make the decisions that they did and continue to do?

Well, they had a few books to assist them. One is a widely used publication that helps structure meetings for virtually any group. *Roberts Rules of Order,* the world's most well-known set of meeting guidelines, offers a delineated process for everything from establishing a quorum to taking questions from the public. The others are the 700-page *Ohio Trustees Handbook,* a set of questions and answers designed to interpret the sections of Ohio Code pertaining to townships, and the *Ohio Trustee Sourcebooks,* prepared by an institute at Miami University in conjunction with the Ohio Township Association.

Parliamentary procedure was developed by a "sparely built but gregarious and determined" Army engineer named Henry Martyn Robert after he suffered a profound embarrassment. The story goes that Robert, a deeply religious man, was asked at the last minute to run a meeting at his church. He agreed, but his attempts to maintain order were fruitless, and the meeting plunged into chaos. "His embarrassment was supreme," says one biography. "In all his assignments he had shown himself to be a promising soldier, competent leader, and an outstanding engineer. Yet . . . Robert lost control of the church meeting."

But he needn't take it personally. Robert realized that many meetings across the country operated with the same stumbling inefficiency, and he decided to do something about it. He read all

FIGURE 13. Henry Martyn Robert, later in life after he had recovered from the tragedy of losing control of a church meeting.

he could on official procedure and created his own, finishing the first edition of *Robert's Rules of Order* in 1875.

After a few publishers rejected the book, Robert took it upon himself to print 4,000 copies of the pocket-sized guide. It was relatively easy to understand and sufficiently comprehensive, establishing "a hierarchy of guiding principles that ensures order while protecting and advancing democratic principles." Meeting attendees everywhere took to the book, and by the beginning of the twentieth century, *Robert's Rules of Order* became the go-to guide for running meetings.[17] Robert retired from the U.S. Army in 1901

---

17. "But the average person doesn't have to know all this to be able to function effectively in most ordinary meetings, or even to chair one," the association says. "At least 80 percent of the content of *Robert's Rules of Order* will be needed less than 20 percent of the time." And the association has a puzzling way of talking about its system: "For those that will brave it . . ." one sentence begins. They also say that readers "need not apologize" if they find that reading the book is a "bigger project than [they'd] like to take on."

and spent the last decade of his life writing about parliamentary procedure. The fourth edition of his guide was published a few years before his death in 1923.

The books and the method became a family business. (His grandson, Henry M. Robert III, has served as Parliamentarian of the National Association of Parliamentarians.) His descendants revised and published subsequent editions of the book, advancing with the times with versions on CD-ROMs and e-books. The most recent edition of *Robert's Rules of Order,* its eleventh, boasts almost 700 pages of rules, charts, and illustrations. But one book can't anticipate every technical emergency, so the Robert's Rules Association often acts as the arbiter on complex or obscure procedural concerns, encouraging meeting fans to submit questions about protocol to be answered.

For Ohio-specific questions, trustees consult the *Ohio Trustees Handbook* or the *Ohio Trustee Sourcebook.* It's no wonder that such guides exist, as Ohio Code gets pretty thorough and it may be hard to keep the regulations straight. One item in Ohio Code, for example, establishes a time of year (the second Monday in January) when the trustees will take inventory of all the materials, machinery, tools, and other supplies, along with establishing a time for cutting noxious weeds, which the trustees are obligated to do before the 20th day of June, August, and, if necessary, September. Another section enjoins any prohibition on the construction of prefab houses on residential lots, while another describes the circumstances in which a township can build a footbridge. (Costs cannot exceed $15,000, and if a bridge straddles the boundaries between townships, either jurisdiction can do work on it.) The code even has a section dedicated to what happens when two candidates in an election have the same name. Lamar Spracklen said that the Ohio Revised Code and the trustee handbooks are the best schooling any public official can get—if you don't know something, simply look it up and there you have it, no matter what it is, officially delineated.

Miami Township elected its first trustees in 1816 and has maintained the same leadership structure since then: three trustees and a fiscal officer (previously called a *clerk*). To become a trustee, a candidate must be a resident of the township (and can reside in either an incorporated or unincorporated part of the township) and a qualified elector.[18] When they take office, the trustees are legally obligated to post a $1,000 bond set by a municipal or county judge to ensure "faithful performance" of trustee duties. Trustees are compensated for their work, but payment amounts differ depending on the township's budget. In Miami Township, with its annual budget of "just a shade under a million dollars," can pay its trustees "not more than $54.01 per day for not more than 200 days," or a maximum of $10,802 per year. Higher budgets, however, do not mean commensurate earnings for the trustees. The budget of nearby Beavercreek Township is approximately $20 million, but its trustees do not earn more than $22,000 per year. Township governments are allowed to offer their employees health and life insurance, provided the insurance policies are the same for everyone, from trustee to road crewman. Miami Township offers health insurance to its employees, though none of the current trustees avail themselves of the opportunity: all three use Medicare, partly because it makes personal financial sense and partly because it saves the township an estimated $900 per month per trustee. "That's one of the good parts of getting old," Mucher said.

Despite the controversies that sometimes arise or the touchy issues that must be attended to, Spracklen said that the trustees, fiscal officer, and other township employees had a great working relationship, the kind that one might expect to develop after so much experience working together. Mucher was elected in 1996, Silliman and Spracklen in 1999, and Crockett in 2001. (In fact, Spracklen and Silliman met for the first time when they were putting up election signs next to each other.) Dan Gochenouer had worked for the township for years before becoming chief road fixer, while Richard Zopf had much experience worked on zoning issues in both the incorporated and unincorporated areas of the township; all in all, to this day the crew has been working in its current formation for at least fifteen years.

---

18. From the Ohio Revised Code: 3503.01 Every citizen of the United States who is of the age of eighteen years or over and who has been a resident of the state thirty days immediately preceding the election at which the citizen offers to vote, is a resident of the county and precinct in which the citizen offers to vote, and has been registered to vote for thirty days, has the qualifications of an elector and may vote at all elections in the precinct in which the citizen resides.

Trustees have their pet projects or areas of expertise. Spracklen, for example, is interested in zoning, while Mucher generally tends to anything cemetery-related; this arrangement means that certain trustees know more about one issue than the other trustees. But the selective knowledge is not a shortcoming for the trustees as a whole, as everyone trusts each other to know what they're doing. Mucher noted that in twenty years of meetings, he couldn't recall ever thinking anyone was undertaking their duties with anything even approaching a partisan slant—taking care of the township is motivation enough. (Township trusteeship is by law a nonpartisan position.)

The camaraderie among the Miami Township trustees "is unusual," Spracklen said, and something not necessarily reflected in Ohio's other townships. Other officials "typically have more tension, ego, desire for personal power. We don't always agree, but I don't lose sleep over it. If there was always a big problem, I wouldn't run again."

Of course, after almost fifteen years in office, one may very well be considered an expert politician, but it bears reiterating that for most of Miami Township's trustees, the trusteeship is the only political office they've ever held. The trustees find themselves in a strange new world, a finely nuanced way of looking at the place that they call home. Whether enervating or energizing, township trustee work is always interesting, as the following examples indicate:

Trustees were presented with two complex issues at their meeting on July 15, 1996. The first involved a property full of trash that no amount of registered letters and attempts at intervention by other county agencies could clean up. The yard of one township resident was so full of junk and refrigerators and old cars that neighbors were worried about the threat it posed to health and safety. The trustees and the county attempted to get in touch with the property owner and tell him he had to get rid of the junk, but the homeowner simply ignored their requests. This put the township in a bind: they wanted the stuff removed, but they couldn't force him to do it. The law stated the cars couldn't be moved unless the homeowner was notified; the homeowner was simply ignoring the letters. Eventually, the township decided to bring a civil suit against the property owner.

It is primarily the threat of a financial penalty or the possibility of losing a precious collection of junk that keeps homeowners from clogging up their property with such unsightly assemblages. But even with official notice that proceedings will take place against a property, it is sometimes difficult for a township to follow through with the threat. A township is responsible for the cost of storing or removing the items, which, in the case of a few acres full of cars and parts of old machines, is not at all cheap. The township can get a lien put on the property but wouldn't recoup its expenses until the property is sold or the homeowner dies, a gamble that likely wouldn't work out in the township's favor, at least not in the short term.

The same 1996 meeting brought another unusual problem to the trustee table. The township had set up an "oil igloo" in a municipal parking lot in Yellow Springs in which residents could deposit old motor oil for proper disposal. However, the township had to pay for the disposal of a substantial amount of what was considered hazardous waste after someone poured paint into the igloo, which, when dumped in the truck sent to collect it, contaminated the entire truckload of oil. The "public [apparently] doesn't appreciate the service" said then-president Dale Reed, as the paint incident was the second time a truckload of old oil was contaminated by someone pouring the wrong liquid into the igloo. The first time it was antifreeze, but both were costly errors (or pranks) that made the trustees "re-evaluate their commitment to the service," as frequently paying to dispose of hazardous waste was not something they wanted to include in their budget.

Speaking of contamination, Miami Township is host to a few businesses that have spotty environmental records. Beginning in the 1950s and continuing into the early 1990s, employees of three companies—Yellow Springs Implements (YSI), Vernay Laboratories, and Morris Bean & Company—disposed of hazardous chemicals by simply dumping them on the ground. Once word of the pollution got around, citizens advocated for the testing of area wellheads, as all of the companies were located near the underground water table that serves Yellow Springs and much of Miami Township. Tests proved that traces of potentially carcinogenic chemicals were present in the water supply.

Specialty metal fabricator eponymously named Morris Bean & Company—the founder of the company—maintained a recalcitrant posture when it came to acknowledging culpability, even though their wastewater was verifiably pouring into sinkholes on the property, which in turn filtered down to the water table. The company patched the sinkholes with concrete mesh, but then new sinkholes formed. In order to address the new sinkhole, the company said it wanted to tie into the Yellow Springs sewer system to treat its wastewater, which at the time was being collected in seldom-serviced tanks on the company's property that spilled over into the sinkholes. Political and financial considerations have left the situation still unresolved. Many feel that the company is holding the village hostage by making the only option either tying into the sewer system or leaving the wastewater treatment up to Morris Bean & Company, who thus far have not been very good about managing their effluent.

Vernay, a company that specializes in flow control systems, has been even worse about acknowledging its role in creating pollution. The practice of dumping toxins in the dirt continued unabated until neighbors brought a lawsuit against the company in the early 1990s. As of 2016, no resolution was in sight, as the parameters for the cleanup efforts were still being debated via lawsuit and counter-lawsuit. Vernay has since left the area, and the enormous lot adjacent to where its property once stood has remained vacant for more than two decades, as nobody can determine if it is safe to use or not or, if it is not safe for general purposes, what an acceptable use might be.

On the other hand, YSI, a developer of water-quality monitoring systems, has historically been much better about addressing the contamination wrought by its previous employees, even if those efforts were mandated by the EPA. The YSI saga began essentially by accident: in 2001, the EPA was investigating Vernay's illegal dumping and found toxic compounds, but they were not the toxic compounds used by Vernay. They were traced to the YSI campus, and the Ohio EPA began investigating the extent of YSI's contamination shortly thereafter. Mandatory cleanup activities began in 2006. YSI injected into the soil a vegetable-oil-based product called CAP18, which grows microbes that metabolize the toxins in the soil and water. The CAP18 would theoretically follow the same soil pathways as the contaminants and eat them. (Trustee Chris Mucher was involved with a citizen's committee overseeing the remediation efforts. This committee was given a grant by YSI to hire a consultant to independently assess YSI's approach, in order to make sure the company's cleanup efforts were actually legitimate.) Decreasing levels of contamination showed that the CAP18 was eating the pollution as expected, and a petition to close the remediation efforts was submitted to the EPA in spring 2016 as the toxins were apparently metabolized into acceptable limits.

But while the successful remediation was obviously good news, the situation presented some interesting bureaucratic headaches for Miami Township trustees. As part of YSI's efforts to appease the residents whose well-sourced water was affected by the pollution, the company agreed to pay to install water lines to their homes, which were all located in the unincorporated area of Miami Township. The trustees, who are all interested to some degree in maintaining the "rural character of the township," were worried that water lines providing drinking water and fire protection would spur development in areas where there previously wasn't any. "Zoning restrictions change when utilities are present," said township zoning czar Richard Zopf.[19]

Township control over mining and mineral rights has been turned over to public utility commissions over the past few years. According to Ohio Code, a township may not tamper with the operations of public utilities or cell phone towers on its land; once a mining operation or cell tower is in place, there is little a township can legally do to legislate it. However, before such an operation is set up, a township can make the parameters under which mining is allowed so narrow that it basically can't happen. Mucher said that while the trustees can't prohibit cell towers from being constructed, Miami Township's code has a thirty-page section outlining when and how they can go up. He noted with some satisfaction that his township's regulations for cellular towers are some of the strictest in the state. (The strength of these policies

---

19. An interesting subproblem developed as part of the YSI process, one that spoke for the varying levels of visibility accorded private citizens and public servants. The committee overseeing the wellhead cleanup efforts sent an anonymous survey to area officials and the residents in the wellhead area to gauge their opinion of the water quality and cleanup effort. However, the trustees unanimously agreed not to fill out the form in public session, as their answers would become part of the public record, making their private opinions known to the world. The opinions expressed about water cleanup were probably not so personal that they would in any way affect the lives of the trustees if exposed, but that wasn't the point; the larger point was one of being entitled to privacy or not, or where the line gets drawn. The trustees stressed they were not urging private citizens to refuse to complete the forms.

was recently undermined when the state ruled that townships had control over cell towers only in residentially zoned areas and nowhere else.)

The trustees' efficiency and comity also helps them work through some of the more emotional township issues, as some of life's most sacred processes have to be dealt with on a bureaucratic level. The trustees oversee the operations of the township's cemetery and fire department, the particulars of which are discussed at almost every trustee meeting. With such duties in mind, the trustees were ready to move the September 9 meeting on to discuss graver matters. Having opened the meeting, passed some resolutions, and discussed the correspondence received by the township, trustees addressed the next items on the September 9 agenda: reports on the recent goings-on of the fire department and the township's cemeteries.

CHAPTER 5

The Fire Department Report

Miami Township Fire-Rescue (MTFR) is a primarily volunteer
department consisting of three full-time employees, eight part-
time employees, and 38 volunteer members. We provide Advanced
Life Support (ALS) emergency medical transportation, fire prevention and suppression, rescue services, and safety education to the
residents and over 1 million annual visitors to our service area.
MTFR responds to emergencies in a 24 square mile area, encom-
passing the villages of Clifton and Yellow Springs and the unincorporated parts of Miami Township. This area includes John Bryan
State Park, the Clifton Gorge State Nature Preserve, the Glen
Helen Ecology Institute and Antioch College. Services are provided from two fire stations, located in Clifton and Yellow Springs.

—MTRF website, http://www.mtfr.org/

The Fire Department Report was item number (5) on the September 9 agenda. In addition to mentioning the fifty-eight EMT and
twenty-four fire incidents the department had responded to since
the last meeting, Mucher said the MTFR would be having a char-
ity car wash the upcoming weekend. Other than that, there wasn't
a whole lot to report, or at least not a lot that the trustees were
directly involved in themselves. The trustees appoint a fire chief
and are generally content to leave the firefighting to the experts.

Nevertheless, the trustees manage the fire department, and,
as public servants (and residents of the township), they have a
vested interest in its operations. The township's fire department
is a concern particularly close to trustee Mark Crockett. At one
point, his son and daughter were both volunteers with MTFR,
and he wanted to ensure there was a trustee who was fire-depart-
ment-friendly. His kids encouraged him to run for trustee, and he
mounted the campaign that resulted in his first term in 2001. It

FIGURE 14. Trustee Mark Crockett. Photo courtesy of the *Yellow Springs News*.

was a narrow victory, and one that initially appeared to be a loss. He lost by eight votes until the mail-in ballots were counted, and it turned out he had actually won by four votes.

Crockett had no experience in running a fire department. In fact, in the first candidate debate, he said that his strategy was to listen to what everyone else had to say and repeat it. (He wasn't able to do this, however, as the emcee called on him first.) Once elected, he said it took him about two years to learn even the scope of the trustees' duties. Things come up you would never in a million years expect, he said, for example, leveling out a grave. There's more to it than just throwing in dirt and tamping it down, and you have to take time to find out about practical things like that, he said. However, he got the swing of it and slowly took on pet projects—like MTFR's concerns—and explored other issues that especially interested him.

At one point, Crockett was on the sidewalk committee and was its youngest member. He's sixty-seven, he said, and the only one on the sidewalk committee who's still alive. One of his favorite committees was the community resources committee, which assessed the different ways in which the community could generate revenue. One of the projects of the community resource committee concerned developing plans for a business park. The park was to be used as manufacturing and business headquarters and currently hosts the campus of Antioch University Midwest. The land was originally the township's and was annexed by Yellow Springs.

But one of the more complex duties of a trustee is maintaining the fire department. MTFR has firehouses in Yellow Springs and Clifton; it answers an average of 686 EMT calls and 319 fire calls annually.[20] The company is staffed primarily by volunteers, who work an average of 13,594 hours per year. (Of those hours, 7,149 are spent on fire incidents, in training, or at special events.) The department's average response time is three minutes and seventeen seconds. The lowest average response time was in 2012: two minutes and thirty-five seconds.

Previously operated by Yellow Springs, the area's fire department came under the jurisdiction of Miami Township in 1951. Yellow Springs felt it wasn't up to the task and ceded control, as the history between the village and the fire department was not especially cordial. The first provision for the purchase of firefighting equipment was passed in 1867, but it wasn't until 1873 that the village bought four fire extinguishers and five leather buckets. Nearby jurisdictions would come by railroad or buggy to help Yellow Springs with any fires, but these modes of travel were in no way timely (horses "speeding one mile an hour" came from Springfield). In addition, other cities were left unprotected when surrounding jurisdictions came to help Yellow Springs. Owing to the fairly frequent and fairly serious conflagrations that would consume the village, the Yellow Springs fire department went through some organizational changes in 1896 to make it more effective and to staunch the rising insurance costs for downtown buildings. (A huge fire broke out downtown in 1891 and then again in

20. From the department's FAQs:

> **Do you get cats or other pets out of trees?** Generally, no. It is rare to find a cat skeleton in a tree. We recommend placing the pet's food in an open container at the base of the tree and wait[ing] for it to come down.
>
> **It's two o'clock in the morning. Why are you using your sirens?** Ohio law requires that we use both lights and sirens when responding in an emergent manner. Sorry.

(http://www.mtfr.org/faq.html, accessed November 26, 2017)

1895, destroying all but one building. The blazes were covered by a short-lived newspaper called, appropriately, the *Yellow Springs Torch*.) The village bought an eighty-gallon Howe Hand Pumper fire truck as part of these changes, and soon they were able to brag that they could "put out any ordinary fire." MTFR still displays this old vehicle, which was originally hand-drawn and was later retrofitted to be horse-drawn. "This apparatus has required little or no maintenance in the last 115 years," says the department's website. "Just goes to show they don't make them like they used to." Today, MTFR's fleet includes two ambulances, a pickup fitted for firefighting, a pickup for paramedics, and two large fire trucks, including Engine 82, a 2010 Seagrave Marauder II, which is capable of pumping 1,250 gallons of water per minute.

The budget of the Miami Township Fire and Rescue is one of the township's highest, as no other township duty requires the equipment and vehicles that fighting fires does. These expenses are paid in part by revenue collected from charging for EMT transportation. An ambulance ride starts at around $400 and costs $9 per mile to the hospital, though township residents who don't have insurance will not be billed for the service. MTFR's expenses are also paid for by real estate taxes in the township. Greene County collects these taxes and redistributes them to individual municipalities like Miami Township. The township presents a budget to the county every year, and monies are distributed accordingly. Fiscal officer Margaret Silliman presents the month's bills at each meeting, and each item on the bill has a breakdown of what revenues are being used to pay it.

The fire department is also the township department with the most safety concerns and liability issues. As such, the fire department is constantly negotiating with the trustees about equipment upgrades. But as MTFR Fire Chief Colin Altman pointed out, it's not about new stuff for the sake of having new stuff. Outdated equipment can be dangerous and cumbersome, while new equipment is designed to make things easier, lighter, faster, and safer for firefighters.

Fighting fires is a monumental task, but so is the day-to-day routine of MTFR firefighters. They have to balance the needs of the department with their pledge to help their fellow township residents when in distress, no matter what. Take 2003, for example. The year was not especially remarkable in the number of fires the department fought or the scope of their emergencies; rather, the year illustrates the diverse concerns and nuanced issues regularly tackled by the department.

The year 2003 got off to a teetotaling start, and not just because nonalcoholic eggnog was served at the December 16, 2002, trustees meeting. Chief Altman announced that the department would participate in a drug-free workforce program through the Bureau of Workers' Compensation in order to get a discount on their workers' comp insurance premiums. The first round of discounts would be achieved by adopting a policy of drug testing all incoming employees. After a year, a further discount would be applied when the department adopted a policy of randomly drug testing 10 percent of its employees throughout the year. Eventually, the department could get a 20 percent discount on its premiums by doing more frequent testing.

In March, the MTFR turned an annoyed glare toward the students of Antioch College, who were responsible for almost twenty fire alarms in a two-month period, far more than the three or four false alarms per year that can be expected at the average community building. The alarms were triggered by little more than smoke caused by incense or excessive smoking of cigarettes, but the process of addressing a potential emergency is the same anytime a call comes in: the firefighters suit up in over forty pieces of equipment and roar out of the station. The MTFR had done this 103 times for the college over the past year.

"The situation is getting completely out of hand," Altman said. "A vast number of alarms are set off by students not thinking, and there is very little consequence or oversight for their actions."

Because of all of the trouble and the evident frequency of the nonemergency alarms, Chief Altman decided to start charging the college $300 for every false alarm that happened within thirty days of the one that preceded it; the college paid $2,400 in fines between January and March 2003.

It was not only a matter of time and resources for MTFR but one of safety for Antioch students, who had taken to ignoring the alarms because so many turned out to be false. It was also a matter of principle, as Antioch is a tax-exempt institution that does not pay the property tax that helps fund MTFR. As such, the college informed the fire department that it didn't have to pay any fine levied on it by a public institution. The Greene County fire marshal stepped in and said that because people lived there, MTFR firefighters would be the ones protecting them if there was an emergency. When Chief Altman sent a letter to the college stating as much, the trustees said they had Altman's back, and the college was required to pay any fine they were given. MTFR used the proceeds from the fines to buy a new defibrillator.

A few weeks later, the firefighters of MTFR got ready to cheer on one of their own in one of the toughest of all sports. In April, volunteer firefighter Laura Kerr had her first game as a professional football player with the Columbus Flames, a team in the National Women's Football Association. Kerr, the team's middle linebacker and defensive captain, had a pretty busy life: she was a volunteer with MTFR and a full-time firefighter and paramedic in Fairborn, and she attended at least three football practices per week.

"I love the hitting," she said. "There's something unique about the collisions that take place on the football field."

Although the players had an incredibly rigorous schedule and had to pay some expenses out of pocket—the league was in its infancy, so players had to pay for bus fare to games and act as sales reps to get sponsors for the team—being able to play football was nothing less than the actualization of a lifelong fantasy for Kerr. Growing up, she played football nonstop, but there was never the chance for her to play on an organized team; consequently, she never considered herself a football player, even though it was the game she loved most. As a member of the Flames, however, she felt different. I'm not just any athlete, she said; I'm a professional football player.

Firefighting was crucial to her making the cut to be on the team. The physical strength it requires to be a firefighter gave her a leg up in plowing through fellow players like she would plow through the door of a burning building. Moreover, she said, the intense concentration required to respond to an emergency situation helped her focus her adrenaline while on the field. Her MTFR colleagues took some pride in having such an athlete among their ranks. They were able to see firsthand how proudly she wore the linebacker mantle when she came into work one day in her football finery, bedecked in her jersey and shoulder pads, helmet by her side, and posing for photos with the chief and her fellow firefighters. So meaningful is the game to Kerr that she said she would leave most anything for the chance to play professional football, including giving up her dream of owning a small farm somewhere in the township. Until then, however, she first had to endure the "unbearable wait" for the season opener: not only the Flames' first game of the season but the first game of a person who knew she was born to play football.

The following month, May 2003, MTFR held a barbeque fundraiser to help raise the $10,000 needed to buy a thermal-imaging camera. Those who have ever seen an action movie should be familiar with what appears on the screen: hot items glow red while cooler items are blue. When used in a fire setting, the camera enables the firefighters to see the source of fire or hidden pockets of flame, as well as locate people inside buildings or wandering around outside after a fire. Altman called the cameras the best things for firefighters since the hose. At that point, the department's camera was so old that the model had been discontinued three years before; the old camera was permanently affixed to a helmet and weighed more than fifteen pounds, with an unimpressive display. Batteries had to be ordered from the U.K. and took two months to arrive. Fortunately the department already had $4,300 set aside for the new camera, so raising the remainder was a less daunting task than trying to raise the $25,000 needed to buy the first camera. Fundraiser attendees were invited to use the then-current camera to get a sense of what infrared fire looks like by pointing it at the flaming grill. Trustee Mark Crockett's blues band Natural Facts played at the event.

In August, just in time for school to begin, the trustees approved the presence of high school students as volunteers on MTFR runs. High school students were not allowed to run into burning buildings, but they did provide important ground support by getting equipment and hoses ready. Nevertheless, the trustees suspended high school volunteers for a year on the advice of their risk management advisor. But MTFR soon felt the loss of five volunteers and were worried that future volunteer numbers would be in jeopardy because high school recruits often continued on as full-time volunteers when they graduated.

After consulting with a handful of local and national fire stations, the trustees voted to re-allow high school students to be volunteers. MTFR found a way to address the issue from an insurance standpoint by becoming an Explorer site for the Boy Scouts

Learning for Life program, which provides participants with $15 million worth of insurance for their activities. The decision provided more manpower for the department and opened a door of opportunity for adventurous teenage souls. "Cadets want to experience the real thing, not sit around the fire house and hear stories about fighting fires and helping emergency victims," said Chris Triplett, an MTFR volunteer who got his start as a cadet.

MTFR's Power Cot

One of MTFR's more recent purchases is designed not only to better assist those in the township but also to preserve the lives—and backs—of first responders.

A significant percentage of injuries sustained by firefighters stem from straining their backs, specifically while carrying people on stretchers. In addition to the weight of the person being transported, the average stretcher (cot) weighs around ninety pounds, making for a heavy cargo to carry up- and down-stairs or over obstructions. Chief Altman said the MTFR responds to around 800 calls per year, and 85 percent of those involve transporting someone via stretcher.

Fortunately for those being transported, and very fortunately for the backs of the MTFR crew, the department got a new stretcher that will take some of the strain off of them. The new cot is a brand-new "Power Cot," with a hydraulic lift system capable of hoisting 700 pounds. The modern device—called the Ferno iNʃX (officially pronounced "in-ex," or "INXS" by Altman)— gleams black and fire engine red.

Unlike traditional cots (and even some newer Power Cots), the MTFR's new device is built so that each set of wheels can retract and extend independently of the other. Thus the cot can easily navigate anywhere with a big height differential, such as stairs and the back of an ambulance. One set of wheels will extend, touch the ground, and be followed in kind by the other side, eliminating the need for the rescuers to carry the entire weight of the cot and its passenger down the stairs. The extendable sides can also be used to step over obstacles like highway dividers. Of course, Altman said, the hydraulics meant the new cot weighed double

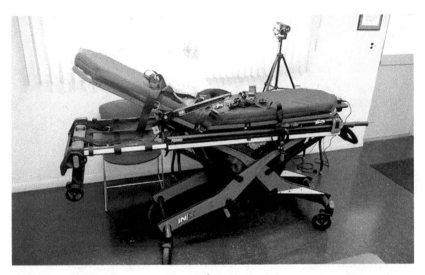

FIGURE 15. MTFR's brand-new Ferno iNʃX Power Cot. Photo by Dylan Taylor-Lehman, courtesy of the *Yellow Springs News*.

a normal cot, but the greatly reduced need for lifting made this extra weight manageable.

Altman saw the iNʃX at a trade show in 2015 and was sufficiently impressed that he decided to use some of the department's annual budget to purchase one. The cot's cost was as impressive as its capabilities: one iNʃX Power Cot costs around $30,000. Fortunately, and remarkably, one-third of the bill was footed by the surprise donation of an anonymous citizen, "who just came into the department one day and wrote a $10,000 check."

The crew learned all about the cot's features, though at the time of the interview with Altman, he said is the only one who hasn't gotten to play with it at length yet. (Cot rides for pleasure are unfortunately not available to the public.) The manufacturer was going to send a rep to do a training seminar not long after it was purchased. The cot, like most of the other emergency and fire equipment used by MTFR, is inspected and serviced every six months, for liability purposes, Altman said. "Liability issues have gotten more complex as the years go by, just like equipment has," he said.

Previous cots could be cleaned by "just by hosing them down," but the cleaning process appropriate for the Power Cot is still to be determined. Altman did note, however, that they have a "barrel of special wipes with cleaning product that kills almost every-thing," and these will probably suffice.

The new cot arrived at MTFR before its partner, a brand-new ambulance. New ambulances are made to order (two of the coun-try's roughly thirty ambulance manufacturers are in Ohio), and one of the last steps was fitting the ambulance with a rack specifically for the cot, which will allow it to slide in neatly and securely. The mount will also serve as a way to charge the cot, as the hydraulic system is battery-powered.

Altman said MTFR aims to buy a second Power Cot in the future and would have one of its other ambulances fitted to accommodate it as well. The department can apply for a grant to buy a cot through the Bureau of Workers' Compensation. Power Cots are at the top of the list of things to receive BWC grants, owing to the amount of injuries associated with hefting.

When asked if there is a blessing or a welcoming-type cere-mony for such an impressive and helpful piece of equipment, Altman said no. The arrival of the new ambulance will be her-alded with some kind of ritual, he said, but that's because it cost $190,000.

Extended interviews with MTFR Chief Altman and Lieutenant Nate Ayers are located in Appendix B.

New Tech Finds Old Graves

A Few Days in Miami Township's "Most Visible Cemetery"

> Planning for the end of your life is a difficult undertaking.
> However, making advance arrangements is a gift to the fam-
> ily members you are leaving behind. Grief at the time of a
> loss is enough for anyone to deal with, without the addi-
> tional burden of making plans and filling out paperwork.
>
> —Glen Forest Cemetery website,
> http://www.miamitownship.net/cemetery_glen.html

Miami Township operates two cemeteries—the Glen Forest Cemetery and the Clifton Cemetery—and cemetery upkeep falls under
the purview of the trustees. The trustees oversee what will be the
final resting place of many area residents—including their own
neighbors and friends—and they carry out this duty with the
expected solemnity due the occasion. In this way, township trustees are officially touched by every death that happens within the
township's boundaries.

As such, cemetery business is a regular part of trustee meetings. The trustees tend to the grounds and schedule burials, and
they maintain the records of who was and will be buried there.[21]

---

21. At the meeting on September 8, 2004, for example, the trustees discussed
the $3,000 they had set aside for upkeep of cemetery headstones. (The town-
ship makes some of its money for cemetery upkeep from the sale of burial
plots.) Dozens of headstones had taken on a tilt or had completely fallen off
their bases. The trustees had been repairing a few at a time, starting with the
eight headstones in most dire need of repair. It was a much-needed improve-

Chris Mucher oversees the operations of the Glen Forest Cemetery while Lamar Spracklen sits on the board of the Clifton Cemetery, a duty he shares with a trustee from Greene Township, as the Clifton Cemetery straddles two jurisdictions. Previously, Spracklen didn't have a huge interest in cemeteries, but because his family has longtime roots in Clifton, he grew to feel some responsibility for keeping the resting places of his forebears in good shape.

Both cemeteries date back at least a century and a half. The cemeteries are quiet, verdant locations, home to the smooth-edged headstones and shaded paths characteristic of small-town graveyards. In the most grandiose sense, the cemeteries reflect the cycle of life and death and all of the intrigue that happens in between. But most cemetery business is less existential and more bureaucratic in nature.

Item (7) on the September 9 agenda was concisely titled "Cemetery Business." Nothing beyond this topic was listed, but that was Dan Gochenouer's department, and he knew what he had to report. In addition to being on the road crew, Gochenouer was sexton of the township's cemeteries, overseeing all their maintenance and grave-digging needs.

"Two ashes, two burials, one ash in Clifton," Gochenouer said. "No progress on the disinterment, though."

"Ashes" was shorthand for cremation, and the disinterment involved a body in the Glen Forest Cemetery that had to be excavated and moved 100 feet down the row. It seemed that successive sextons had double-sold the property. A new burial had been scheduled at the same plot, where there were already remains, and the new tenant got precedence. But this sort of mix-up isn't uncommon for old cemeteries, Mucher said. It was most likely an accident, as records were bound to get lost or mixed up over the years. But mix-ups aside, the cemetery had been fairly calm, Gochenouer said. "You'll get a few burials in a row and then it'll go dead," he said. "If you'll pardon the pun." The officials took the disinterment update in stride and groaned at the wisecrack. Mucher commented that the hedges Gochenouer trimmed looked nice.

The update taken care of, the officials moved on to discuss the premier piece of cemetery business at the September 9 meeting,

---

ment, as Lamar Spracklen noted that none of the trustees could even recall the "last time any effort was put into headstone repair."

which did happen to involve missing records. A few weeks before the meeting, ground-penetrating radar discovered the remains of thirty-five unknown people on Glen Forest's grounds. Nobody knew who they were, but they could make an educated guess.

The Glen Forest Cemetery, the "township's most visible cemetery," has been in use since the 1820s. The cemetery caps off the north end of Yellow Springs and extends east and west on both sides of Route 68. The township began caring for the 750 gravesites of the original five-acre cemetery at the beginning of 2013, taking over for trustees of the Glen Forest Cemetery Association who realized, as George Eliot put it, the "new spring brings no new shoots out on the withered tree." In other words, the cemetery trustees wanted to ensure that someone would look after the cemetery once they themselves had also passed into the infinite beyond, and so they passed the torch to the township.

The cemetery was close to capacity, and the township decided to expand the cemetery to the land across the street, doubling its size. (If a township wanted to open a new cemetery, it had to be voted on and approved by residents, but old cemeteries could be expanded without a vote.[22]) The new cemetery would have space for 900 new markers, roads, and benches. Half of the land would be for traditional burials, and half would be for natural burials. In the latter case, embalming is prohibited (unless with approved nontoxic products), and bodies can be wrapped in nothing but a "shroud, quilt or blanket or be placed in a burial container," provided it doesn't contain synthetic materials. The accommodation of green burials was something Mucher had pushed for, a pet project he had initiated that was seen through to success.

Expansion aside, there was some land still available within the borders of the original cemetery. The township decided to use it for approximately 300 new plots, and this is where the mystery bodies were found.

---

22. Also, according to the *Ohio Township Handbook*, it's possible that you can be buried on your own property. "Most bodies are buried in established cemeteries, but burial on private land in Ohio may be possible. Before conducting a home burial or establishing a family cemetery, check with the county or town clerk for any local zoning laws you must follow. If you bury a body on private land, you should draw a map of the property showing the burial ground and file it with the property deed, so the location will be clear to others in the future."

FIGURE 16. A standard "baby carriage," ground-penetrating radar apparatus.

In summer 2015, Mucher began updating the cemetery's records in preparation for the new sites. He squared extant registers with those in the dusty old journals and notebooks that came with the cemetery when the township took over. Mucher digitized the notebooks and ledgers, entering a carpal-tunnel-inducing 7,000 pieces of data on "professional cemetery software."

At the same time that the plan for new plots and the record keeping was underway, Mucher attended a cemetery maintenance seminar. He came across the booth of a company called GPRS (Ground Penetrating Radar Systems) offering ground-penetrating radar (GPR), a technology typically used to find buried utilities or reinforcements in concrete. But the company was at the seminar because it had a similar application in cemeteries—to search for unknown items before land was used. Many of the records for the land that the trustees had set aside were lost or nonexistent, so Mucher truthfully didn't know what was under it. Perhaps figuring this out would be a good idea, he thought. The technology was also much more affordable than he realized, so he set up an appointment with Dayton GPRS rep Nate Kollar to ensure that nothing was buried, intentionally or otherwise, in the areas earmarked for the new graves.

Kollar scanned the designated areas in Glen Forest. Using the GPR apparatus was like "pushing a baby carriage," Mucher said, an incongruous image for a cemetery but one that was nonetheless quite accurate, as the radar is in fact pushed around in a small carriage. The GPR process is fairly simple, Kollar said. Radar pen-

etrates up to two feet in concrete applications and up to ten feet
in soil, where the company says its radar is accurate to within
six inches of the center of the object and within 10 percent of
its depth. When anything is found, blips show up on the screen
attached to the radar unit, giving the operator real-time results
while searching.

Because organic materials disintegrate over time, GPRS wasn't
looking specifically for human remains or coffins. The radar detects
underground "void cavities," or strange underground pockets, created around burial containers that have disintegrated.

Cemetery work constitutes only about 1 percent of GPRS's
business, Kollar said, but he looked forward to those jobs. "I
could go about scanning cemeteries every day," he said. The intrin-
sic peace of any cemetery, and being left alone to work, provide
a respite from the noise of a bustling construction site. Nevertheless, Kollar did his work efficiently, not getting too caught up in
the solitude. Mucher and Gouchenour said they were surprised
at how quickly and effortlessly the process was completed. The
entire cemetery was "scanned in half a day," said Mucher. The
results were equally surprising—the radar system picked up evidence of thirty-five bodies, twenty-five of which were buried in
areas allocated for future use. The occupied plots were promptly
removed from the list of available sites, and the interred were left
to continue resting in peace. The rest of the new sites were made
available for sale.

"The discovery brings peace of mind," said Mucher. "We could
have sold that gravesite and would have found someone there
when we went to dig for the new owner."

But the detection, of course, begs one to ask who these people
might be. It turns out there are a few centuries' worth of possibilities. Greene County archivist Robin Heise said use of the cemetery
goes back to 1823, before it was even an official cemetery. Leg-
end has it that 1823 was the year of Glen Forest Cemetery's first
burial, when a young girl passing through the area with her family
via stagecoach died and was buried under a tree on the grounds.
("Unfortunately, there is no marker at this grave and the name
of the family has been forgotten," says the cemetery's website.)
According to the deed accompanying the sale of the cemetery to
the village, the area was to be used "exclusively for mortuary purposes" starting in 1873.

Heise got out a map of the cemetery from 1922 to illustrate why there may be more graves than are accounted for. Cemeteries typically have an area designated for the destitute, she said, and it's possible that that many of the newly discovered remains belong to people who were too poor to have a headstone, or even proper records. However, the twenty-five bodies were found in scattered locations around the cemetery and not in the low-lying area alongside Cemetery Street, an area that Heise said would have been earmarked for a paupers' graves due to its propensity for flooding.

Either way, Heise said, maps are only as good as the records they are based on. She pointed out an area in the northwest side of the cemetery that the 1922 map had delineated as "Old Graves," with no further explanation given. Evidently, records were scare even 100 years ago. But it's not surprising that records are often incomplete in old cemeteries such as Glen Forest. The physical records may have been lost or destroyed over time. Caretakers would often keep a cemetery's ledger at home, Heise said, but when the caretakers died, nobody would realize what the ledgers were for, and someone likely threw them out.

However, there may yet be some clue as to whose remains they may be. In poring over the records, Mucher also found record of 400 burials, complete with names and other identifying information but no indication of where the people were actually buried. "Four hundred is not a guesstimate—there are four hundred official burial records that don't correspond [to any of the claimed sites]," he said. Part of the plan was to put the data online so people could research burials themselves, which may eventually match the records with the anonymous gravesites.

By spring 2016, Mucher was almost done with the cemetery database update he began the year before. He said he had "memorialized 7,800 burials" in the process, not only entering the information contained in cemetery records for each grave but tracking down other biographical information about the interred from old documents and official sources (or even visiting the grave itself to get a birth date) if such information wasn't listed in the cemetery's records. The trustees divide up township tasks as they come, and Mucher took on the task of updating records before he knew what he was getting into.

Despite the work, Mucher said the upside to this mystery is that, as of six months before the September 9 meeting, nobody had even known that these people existed.

"They're not alive again, but they are back among the recorded people," he said.

An Account of the Township's Murders

Some places speak distinctly. Certain dank gardens cry
aloud for a murder; certain old houses demand to be
haunted; certain coasts are set apart for shipwrecks.

—Robert Louis Stevenson, *Memories and Portraits*

Ohio Code holds that a township government may establish its
own police force, but Miami Township has not taken this route,
opting instead to utilize the law enforcement services of the
Greene County Sheriff's Department, which has an obligation to
provide such services to any unincorporated areas of the county
not served by their own police agency. Even though the township
utilizes the sheriff's department, the trustees don't have much official interaction with it; both entities rely on each other to do their
respective duties. In other words, when crime occurs in the township, the trustees don't have many explicit responsibilities in terms
of assisting with or conducting an investigation. Naturally, all of
the township's resources would be at law enforcement's disposal
if need be, for when a tragic death occurs close to home—in one
gruesome township case, literally right in someone's own backyard—the entire area feels the injustice intensely and wants to
bring the responsible party to justice. While a generally peaceful
and low-crime area, Miami Township has had its share of violence, stemming from jealousy, love, imagined slights, or simple
malevolence. But such is the circle of death and life, an Ourobo-
ros that precedes every trustee's tenure and has been a fact of life
since the township's inception.

In fact, humans being humans, Miami Township's first murder was committed shortly after it was founded. In November 1809, William Catrill was accused of murdering the child he had fathered with his wife's sister. He is said to have killed the child and thrown the body into a hogpen, presuming that the animals would remove all traces of the crime. The child's body lay untouched, and Catrill was arrested, tried, and convicted, though he "escaped the extreme penalty" of death thanks to a recent change in state statute.

One of the ghosts of Miami Township is said to reside in the Glen Forest Cemetery. Like the Catrill story, the tale also involves a husband who fell in love with his wife's sister. In December 1863, the body of Caroline Umbenhour was found in the Glen Forest Cemetery, "lifeless as the clay." The case can "hardly find a parallel in the annals of crime," as the body of James Monroe, the murderer, was found naught but a few paces away, passed out after suffering self-inflicted wounds. Umbenhour was the sister of Monroe's wife and had borne him a child outside of marriage, as both were "believers in the baneful airs of free love." The *Xenia Sentinel,* published from 1863 to 1865, reported that Umbenhour was "determined to discontinue the unholy and illicit intercourse" and had accepted the marriage proposal of another gentleman. She told Monroe that "only death" could stop the marriage, and he took her at her word. He then tried to cut his own throat but failed to cut deep enough and so attempted to open the wound with his fingers. The pain was excruciating and the experience so disgusting that he passed out and was found facedown in the cemetery. Monroe was convicted of murder and died not long after, killed not by the state but by being caught in the machinery of the penitentiary's chair factory.

Yet "the record for tragedy was broken" a few years later by a double murder. Lou Keys and George Koogler, a Civil War pensioner, were in love. Their relationship bothered Andy Hunster, the son of local hotel owners, as he was in love with Keys from afar. One night the couple was eating oysters together at the Hunster family's diner. Evidently oysters were a suggestive food to be seen eating with someone in public, and the next morning, Keys and Koogler were found dead. Koogler's wallet was missing and his pockets were flipped inside out. The initial thought was that he was robbed for the $8 pension payment he had just picked up, but a witness identified Hunster as the murderer after recognizing his voice in previous conversation with the lovers. However, there wasn't enough evidence to convict Hunster, and he remained free. But the guilt of the crime ate away at him. A little while later he was said to have burst into a saloon, ashen, saying he saw Keys and Koogler walking hand in hand, singing the love song Koogler always sang to her—years after they died! Robin Heise, of the Greene County Historical Society, found Hunster listed in the 1880 census as an "imbecile," and a 1910 death record lists him dying in an infirmary, apparently consumed by the horror of what he had done. Lou Keys was buried in the Clifton Cemetery, the township's other cemetery.

And in 1915, a winsome naturalist and autodidact named Denman Duncan caught the eye of one Mrs. Haines, whose husband worked at a nearby nursery. Mr. Haines became incensed that his wife marveled at Duncan's apparently superior knowledge of ferns. "Skunk cabbage is all he's ever found," Haines huffed. Jealousy ate at Mr. Hanes, and one night he crept over to Duncan's cabin and killed him with a hatchet. Naturally, this gruesome death has inspired talks of phantasmagoric sightings in the small valley on which Duncan lived, primarily in the form of a phosphorescent fern that he (and Mrs. Haines) liked.

A story in the *Xenia Daily Gazette* (1882–1997), whose "headline ['Murderer Confesses'] is in the size of font that today would be used for major disasters," discussed how police induced Mrs. Haines to confess that she knew who did it. "Her weak point, the one susceptible emotion in her defiant nature, an inherant [sic] love of her mother, was brought to light by the police and by dwelling upon this point they soon had her in tears. 'What would your dead mother want you to tell, what is she whispering now for you to do?' they questioned, and the tears dropped from her eyes in a wave of emotion. 'I'll tell,' she sobbed . . . expressing satisfaction that her soul had been relieved of the terrible burden."

But while deaths consigned to history can be talked about with some level of detachment, contemporary murders are never free of heart-wrenching immediacy. In bigger cities, people read about death and disappearances in the newspaper; only the victims' friends and families feel, for the most part, the full weight of the tragedy, because other connections to victims are too remote. But in a township the size of Miami Township or a town like Yellow Springs, where almost everyone lives within two square miles of one other, the pain is acute. Neighbors cannot help knowing a lot about their neighbors—residents see the same people every day, patronize each others' businesses, attend the same events, and join the same clubs. This proximity can, of course, lend itself to gossip and judgment, but it also means a deep sense of connection, especially when most townspeople are truly concerned for the well-being of those around them. In a small town, even a relatively minor crime like check fraud feels like a betrayal of trust because townspeople have nowhere to hide from the fact that a crime is being committed.

Murder, the most capital of offenses, is an enormous and completely unexpected punch in the collective gut. Somebody got *killed*—you are forced to think about the fact that someone you probably know carried out the act of hurting someone so viciously that a beautiful flame is forever extinguished from the earth, and that the last moments of someone else you probably know were probably moments of agonizing terror and pain. The nefarious action casts a terrible pall, a phantom of fear and distrust whose icy tendrils claw at the township's soul.

In spring 1981, the township was totally beset by these horrific events: a local couple was machine-gunned while on vacation in Hawaii; a man was tied up and stabbed by hitchhikers; and a Yellow Springs man was killed by his son in his own driveway—all in the span of a few months.

John and Michelle Klein were on vacation in Hawaii in March 1981, taking some time for themselves before John began working for a prestigious law firm in Los Angeles. John was a former Yellow Springs resident, where he graduated Yellow Springs High School as a district tennis champ and ran a well-liked community tennis clinic; Michelle was from Michigan and worked as a technical writer in California. For their vacation the two rented an apartment on Kauai and went hiking on March 20. Three days later, the manager of the apartment they had rented reported them missing. The last time they had (possibly) been seen was in a bar the night before. Soon, the car they had rented was found at the base of a trail with Michelle's purse and other belongings undisturbed, so the Klein family arranged a land-and-air search of the area. Eventually, a rescue dog located their bodies in the jungle, about 100 feet off the trail. John was shirtless, both wore hiking boots, and both were riddled with bullets. Nobody knew what happened. "What we need is a witness," said a detective working the case.

The case was reported on by the *New York Times,* who featured the murders as one of a few then-recent incidents that helped curtail tourist traffic to Hawaii. It wasn't just the apparent increase in crime that bothered people but the fact that the Hawaiian defendants in a handful of highly publicized crimes were acquitted. Would-be tourists were worried not only that they would be attacked but that justice wouldn't be served if the assailant was found. In fact, crime had become such an issue that airlines and hotels offered free tickets and rooms to anyone who had to fly back to the state to testify in a trial. The Klein murders were never solved, though one Yellow Springs local speculated—based on what he said was firsthand experience seeing similar operations—that they had stumbled onto some kind of clandestine drug operation and were killed to make sure it stayed secret. There has been no independent verification of this theory, but no matter the cause, the town was burdened with enormous grief at the loss of one of its own.

The truly unexpected happened a few weeks later, when Walt McCaslin III killed his father Walt II in his home on April 17. The son had returned home a few months prior and was living with his dad. McCaslin II was killed in the kitchen with a steak knife "moments before the younger McCaslin was to be transported for admittance into an alcohol abuse program," reported the *Yellow Springs News* at the time. "He apparently panicked at the prospect of being committed to the treatment program." McCaslin III was known to have been behaving strangely and erratically in the days preceding his treatment, to the degree that it was the police who were going to drive him to the program. Just as the attack began, the police arrived and heard McCaslin II's screams. He collapsed on his front stoop as police ran up to the house. The son fled the house and was confronted by officers elsewhere in the neighborhood, upon which he stopped running, threatened to hurt himself, and then plunged the knife into his own stomach. Police maced McCaslin III and then tripped him with a nightstick, after which he was taken to a hospital. He tried to flee the hospital the following night but was tackled in the hallway by a security guard. Friends, colleagues, and readers mourned the elder McCaslin, a veteran of World War II and "a comrade, a gentle raconteur." He had been the arts critic for the *Dayton Journal Herald* for four-teen years and was known as a firm but fair observer, one whose praise was taken very seriously. He was also known as the "aes-thetic conscience" of the community, as his architectural sensibili-ties were well known and often consulted. "He knew excellence by instinct," said one friend.

The startling McCaslin murder was not the last of that difficult spring. On April 26, a twenty-six-year-old Yellow Springs man named Alan Gillespie picked up two "young and well-groomed" hitchhikers while driving near Lafayette, Louisiana. The three rode in relative peace for about forty minutes before one of the hitchhikers pulled a knife on Gillespie and forced him to get in the back seat, whereupon he was tied up and blindfolded. They drove for another hour and pulled over for gas; at that point they started stabbing Gillespie after he tried to readjust how he was sitting. "Lie down and die," they told him. After driving for another hour, the hitchhikers took a series of back roads and finally stopped the car. The Yellow Springer was dragged out onto a dirt road and stabbed in the neck; he played dead, and his assailants drove off. Gillespie was able to wriggle free of his restraints and walk back to the road, where he was found fifteen minutes later and taken to the hospital, where he underwent emergency surgery. He conva-lesced in Louisiana for a few weeks (he had gone to Louisiana for a temporary gig on an oil rig) and then flew home.

Remarkably, upon his return, Gillespie wrote a letter to the *Yellow Springs News* in which he wanted to express the "feel-ing in [his] heart." People often asked him if he was angry about what happened to him, he said, but he didn't feel any anger about the situation; the anger was that of the assailants and not him. In fact, he didn't want to see them sent to prison but wanted them to receive help learning to control their impulses. "Please, to all my brothers and sisters everywhere, join hands as One," he wrote. "Either we work to help one another or it's every man for himself."

Despite Gillespie's admirable entreaties, some humans seem to have a predilection for aggression, one that can strike in the most heinous and bizarre ways. In March 2000, an incident occurred in Costa Rica involving two Yellow Springs college students. These murders eerily reflected the tragedy in Hawaii that had occurred nineteen years before.

Emily Howell, a poet and photographer, was a second-year student at Antioch who came to the school from Lexington, Kentucky. There she met Emily Eagen, a swimmer from Ann Arbor, and the two became fast friends. They hosted a radio program together and celebrated that they were born only four days apart. When Howell went to study in Costa Rica as part of her co-op program, there was no question that Eagen would come visit her. In March 2000, the two Emilys and another Antioch student rented a car and stayed in a cabin in Puerto Viejo. On March 12, Eagen and Howell went to a nearby bar while their friend stayed behind. They never came back and were reported missing the next morning. Not long after, their jeep was found on the side of a rural road; it had been set on fire. In the bushes near the jeep were the bodies of Howell and Eagen, who had both been shot to death. Both were nineteen.

Police determined that the women had been abducted outside a bar and driven to the spot where they were killed. The killing seems to have been a panicky afterthought. After the women had left the bar, the abductors reportedly drove the jeep away with the Emilys in the back seat. When the jeep stalled, Eagen was ordered to strip, which she began doing. Howell was accidentally shot as she struggled in the car. The perpetrators apparently panicked and killed the women on the side of the road. A little while later, the men flagged down a tow truck, which pulled the jeep back onto the road. The tow truck driver was then told at gunpoint to burn the jeep, which he did, and was let go.

Two men were eventually arrested and charged with the murders. A sixteen-year-old, who had recently attacked a security guard with poisonous gas, was seen driving the women's jeep and wearing jewelry taken from Howell. A nineteen-year-old accomplice was arrested soon thereafter. The murder weapon was recovered when two kids turned over the gun that had been thrown out the men's car window. The sixteen-year-old was sentenced to fourteen-and-a-half years in prison while the nineteen-year-old was given seventy years because he was an adult. A third suspect reportedly escaped back to Nicaragua before he could be apprehended.

Many newspaper accounts from the time mention the families' agonizing screams when they were given the news. The families eventually traveled to Costa Rica to claim their daughters' bodies. The Howells also ended up coming back with a new puppy, as the

FIGURE 17. Antioch student Alena Schaim's "Emilys' Garden," a sculpture garden tribute to Emily Eagen and Emily Howell. The sculpture, made out of adobe and cement, was deliberately designed to crumble. Photo by Aaron Zaremsky, courtesy of the *Yellow Springs News.*

Emilys were constantly playing with a litter of seven puppies who knew exactly which cabin door to come to for food and attention. The Emilys were buried, with memorial ceremonies held on campus and their respective hometowns. The Eagen family eventually donated $6,000 they had raised to three schools in rural Costa Rica in Emily's name.

The women were also memorialized on campus. Two redbud trees were planted in their honor, and a student named Alena Schaim created Emilys' Garden as her senior project. Schaim raised money to construct the sculptures and spent more than $5,000 out of pocket on the project. While Schaim didn't personally know the Emilys, she "'fell in love with them' while working on the sculptures."

"I don't necessarily believe in ghosts, but I think they've been watching me work," she told the *Dayton Daily News* in 2003. "I feel that they are with me, and the sculptures are part of me."

There are five figures in a circle in the garden. By design, they are built to crumble, a paean to the immutable truth that we all return to the earth. "The circle represents creations and the revision of both Emilys' lives," Schaim said.

The new millennium continued its depressing beginning with the disappearance of high school senior Tim Lopez in the beginning of 2002, a heartbreaking occurrence made even worse by the fact that no information about his whereabouts surfaced for more than two years.

Lopez was last seen at 10:00 a.m. on January 22, 2002, at the Yellow Springs High School when he signed out for lunch. His girlfriend became worried when he didn't come to pick her up later that day, and after a daylong search, they found his locked car full of his belongings in the parking lot of Glen Helen. The entire area was searched the next day, but nothing that indicated his whereabouts was found. Once it became apparent that no more information could be gleaned from the vehicle, the investigation slowed drastically and eventually stalled. There were many disappearances in Greene County that year, said one sheriff, but "Tim was the only one we couldn't find." The high school held numerous vigils and counseling sessions in an attempt to deal with the "dark cloud" hanging over the school, as another student had briefly gone missing earlier that year (but was later found, safe). Unable to bear the weight of the disappearance and the feeling that her son would "walk through the door at any moment," Lopez's mother sold her home and moved out of state.

It was rumored that Lopez was involved with a drug-dealing racket from Chicago and that his disappearance was likely connected with these activities. Lopez was said to be either connected to or in rivalry with his classmate Michael Rittenhouse, who was rumored to sell ecstasy and carry a gun. The two were previously best friends, but in the manner of fickle high school relationships, Rittenhouse grew to severely dislike Lopez. His dislike was well known, and rumors abounded concerning Rittenhouse's involvement in the disappearance. But it took the arrest of an older peer named Umoja "Iddi" Bakari to help all the tragic pieces fall into place. Bakari was arrested in Columbus in 2004 and charged with shooting and abducting another person. Though the term *kingpin,* used by the *Columbus Dispatch* and other media outlets to describe Bakari, was certainly a bit sensationalized, he was verifiably connected with fairly serious drug dealing and was facing a considerable amount of jail time, but he was able to leverage his knowledge of what happened to Lopez to reduce the charges against him.

It turned out that it was Rittenhouse who made Lopez disappear, in a particularly grisly and unexpected way. Rittenhouse, alternately described as a nice youth ("he was one of the only young people in town who would say hello to adults") and a transparent sociopath, snuck up on Lopez when he was playing video games in Rittenhouse's basement and killed him by hitting him several times in the head with a baseball bat. The killing was said to have followed a disagreement over the sale of ecstasy, "although it is not clear who was buying the drugs and who was selling, nor the amount of money involved." (People close to Lopez said that a thorough search of his home after he went missing revealed no evidence of drug dealing.) Rittenhouse placed Lopez's body in a storage container in the family's garage for ten days, where he dismissed concern over the growing smell as a "science experiment gone bad." Fearing discovery, Rittenhouse unsuccessfully tried to burn the body in his garage and then buried Lopez under evergreen bushes in his backyard, right behind a children's play structure.

On February 20, 2004, police obtained a search warrant for Rittenhouse's property, thanks to the information provided by Bakari. Bones were discovered, confirmed as human, and Rittenhouse was promptly charged with murder. A warrant was issued for his arrest, and Rittenhouse turned himself in a few hours later. (An unnamed source who knew Rittenhouse said that he was prone to outbursts and irrational behavior in the years before he was caught, including refusing to take a friend he hit with his car to the hospital, opting instead to put him in the back seat of the car and drive around with him for awhile. The enormity of that secret knowledge must have been unimaginably intense.)

Lopez's mother said her son was treated like the way someone would treat trash. Heartbreaking does not even begin to describe what it's like to think of the person you're closest to in the world, whom you've known for eighteen years, whose jokes and mannerisms are reassuringly familiar, whose future you no doubt take pleasure in imagining, and whose safety you had fretted about time and time again (but he would always return home and apologize for forgetting to call), treated like that. "Tim was not trash," she said. "He was an extraordinary boy who was deeply loved."

But perhaps with some sympathy toward what another local mother was experiencing, Rittenhouse, with the consent of Lopez's parents, pleaded guilty to murder and gross abuse of a corpse, a lesser charge that led to a sentence of fifteen years to life, with the possibility of parole after fifteen years. He was originally charged with aggravated murder and aggravated burglary, charges that would have brought with them the possibility of the death penalty.

Investigators remain convinced that a few other friends knew about the murder, and may have even seen the body, but nobody has come forward with information. (The case took another dark turn when Iddi Bakari committed suicide in jail.) Nobody talks much about what happened that night. The case has been solved, and it appears that most people—family and investigators included—prefer to consign it to memory. "For a few moments I forget he's gone," said Beth Burt, Lopez's girlfriend. "And then I remember and it happens all over again."

Not more than two years later, when the Lopez case was barely resolved, another murder took place in the heart of Yellow Springs. In fact, it was not far from where Lopez was killed, and close to the site of a police shooting a few years later. (It was also the stomping grounds of a preteen criminal who repeatedly broke into his neighbors' houses for fun.) There is a sort of dark energy about the place, a presence neighbors have reportedly felt.

A man named Tim Harris was found dead in his home on December 16, 2004, dead of blunt force trauma to his head. A suspect did not immediately present himself because Harris didn't appear to be involved with any serious criminals or shady dealings. By all accounts, Harris was a helpful, good-natured man who often let friends who were down on their luck stay with him until they got back on their feet. His favorite activities were playing harmonica and pool, his sister said, and she goes to talk to him in a park just outside of Yellow Springs that he used to really like. To make matters worse, the family experienced the death of two aunts, Harris's mother, and the mother of his ex-wife over the next two months.

The defensive wounds on Harris's arms, a bike in the house that didn't belong to him, and cash and jewelry still in a safe made the situation quite perplexing, and then police found Harris's car three months later at a scrapyard in Xenia. This was suspicious, as family members knew Harris was in no position to sell his car for scrap, as he needed it to drive to the construction company where he worked. Perhaps taking a cue from the halting progress of the

Lopez murder, Harris's sister, Cynthia, began keeping a journal the week after he died. In her journal she chronicled conversations she had with people about Harris and the rumors she heard regarding her brother's death in the hope that they would be useful later. But as it would turn out, the time between finding Harris's body and bringing charges against the assailant had less to do with a stalled investigation and more to do with wanting to build the most airtight case against the subject they had in mind, who had been on their radar fairly soon after Harris was found. In fact, there was no rush to arrest because the subject was already in jail.

Authorities learned soon after the investigation started that it was not the first time that Harris had his car stolen. A man named Phillip K. Cordell, also of Yellow Springs, stole Harris's car in January 2004 and sold it to the same scrapyard. Police felt it likely that the murder was the result of a confrontation about the second car, as Harris was well aware of who had stolen it and was understandably furious (and probably embarrassed) that it happened again. Though the two once considered themselves friends, Cordell became the most obvious and only suspect after several people reported he was making strange comments about Harris in the days after he was killed. Two days after Harris's body was found, the police arrested Cordell on an unrelated burglary charge for robbing his own uncle's house. The conviction was a parole violation, and he was sentenced to four years in prison for the robbery, having previously been convicted of a host of other crimes. After a fellow inmate later reported that Cordell had confessed to the murder, a friend of both families agreed to wear a recording device when she visited Cordell in jail. "If anyone gets mad that I did this, I don't care—I did it for Timmy's family," she said of her subterfuge. Cordell was recorded making comments alluding to his responsibility for the killing and was charged with murder. Police ultimately determined that the death was likely accidental, the result of a disagreement that got out of hand and led to Cordell's fatally hitting Harris with an ashtray. Cordell was charged with involuntary manslaughter and was given a five-year prison sentence.

The most recent killing in Miami Township was the shooting of Paul Schenck, a Yellow Springs resident who engaged in a firefight with the more than eighty officers from seventeen jurisdictions who surrounded his house; included in the fight were armored vehicles from the area's SWAT team. At 10:45 p.m. on Tuesday, July 30, 2013, a 911 call was made in which the caller reported that an assault had taken place at a residence on North High Street. Schenck, forty-two, was apparently heavily intoxicated after drinking all day and had put a loaded gun to his head when watching TV with his son. He had been suffering from depression and chronic pain for years and was already distraught after one of his cats was killed earlier that day. A fight broke out when his son Max tried to wrestle the gun away from him, leading to the 911 call to police.

When the two responding officers arrived, Schenck was observed, distraught and bleeding, in the small apartment he lived in behind his parents' house. The officers attempted to get Schenck to open the door but he refused. The police pounded on the door, pushing the already agitated Schenck into a panicked state. At around 10:53 p.m., a volley of gunshots ripped through the inside of the apartment, prompting the officers to run for cover. An officer sent out a "signal 99" over the radio, "an indiscriminate call for assistance" from any officers in the surrounding areas. A fleet of vehicles from all over southwestern Ohio made its way to North High Street. In the meantime, when more local cruisers and MTFR vehicles showed up, Schenck shot at them between ten and fifteen times. An announcement was dispersed that neighbors should vacate their homes. More police arrived, setting up a perimeter around the house and beyond, "in case he tried to flee." A helicopter and armored vehicles also arrived, and Schenck shot at the helicopter when it turned on its spotlights.

It was not the first time Schenck had troubles with firearms and police. More than five handguns and twelve rifles were taken from his home in 2009 at the request of his mother after police responded to a stumbling, severely intoxicated Schenck carrying a loaded gun during a confrontation with a neighbor. Schenck was taken to jail and put on suicide watch. Uta Schenck, Paul's mother, recalled with embarrassment that the SWAT team that showed up to remove the weapons was trailed by a host of news vans broadcasting the incident. Schenck served three years' probation for the incident and completed a substance abuse program, after which he stayed sober for a few years. He and his father agreed to sell his guns to pay legal fees and loans. But a little while later, a court order returned all his guns to him, finding no reason he couldn't have them since he completed a rehab program. Slowly but surely, however, Schenck resumed drinking, and his problems escalated accordingly. His guns did not end up being sold and instead stayed with him in his house.

Schenck was having a rough period in the time leading up to the incident. He was in constant, terrible pain due to back problems and gout and was said to drink heavily in an attempt to alleviate the pain. His two kids were teenagers by the time his apartment was under siege, and he was reportedly distressed at not being able to maintain steady employment to pay child support. But friends and family knew that at heart, Schenck meant well and was a decent guy. He was a gifted artist and cook who designed his own toys and tools. He was known for his camouflage and cool music when he was a teen, and for his love of hiking. At one point, he attended college with the intention of becoming a forest ranger, but anxiety, depression, and ill health unfortunately scuttled those plans. It appeared that the fight with his son or the officers' trying to make entry to his home pushed his distress to irreversible levels.

Officers asked Schenck's parents to draw a diagram of the house and give them the domicile's phone number. An officer attempted to call the sequestered Schenck at least fifty-six times, to no avail. One armored vehicle used its PA system to broadcast a number Schenck could call. Paul's mother was upset that she and his father weren't called in to help negotiate, but it was explained that protocol typically didn't allow civilians to come close to a dangerous active crime scene. Schenck's parents were held at bay while officers tried to surround his apartment.

Schenck appeared to be shooting an AR-15, which typically holds a thirty-round magazine and can be fired as rapidly as the user can pull the trigger. Police contemplated running an armored vehicle into the small apartment to get him to stop shooting, or using gas to knock him out. One officer felt that the sunrise would expose the men hiding nearby and decided to act. The officer got close enough to feel hot pieces of metal dust from Schenck's rifle on his head as he hid under the apartment window. When Schenck stopped shooting, the officer jumped up and fired five times into the window. At 2:21 a.m., a call went over police radio that the subject was down. Neighbors said Schenck shouted, "I love you, and I always will!" before he was killed.

FIGURE 18. The scene outside Paul Schenck's apartment, July 20, 2013. Photo by Matt Minde, courtesy of the *Yellow Springs News*.

Schenck was found dead in the apartment at 4:00 a.m. on Wednesday, July 31. A remote-controlled robot confirmed he had been fatally shot. Schenck was wearing a Kevlar vest and earplugs, with a blood-clot kit, gas mask, and thousands of rounds of ammo at the ready. He had fired 191 shots in an almost 360-degree radius from his home, hitting four nearby homes and numerous police vehicles. One official said that some of the bullets had the potential to travel one mile and still be lethal. Police had fired six shots: five by the officer that ultimately killed Schenck and one by another officer who was disciplined for firing his weapon at the apartment without having a strategic reason to. No officers were injured in the standoff.

Villagers held a candlelight vigil for the tragic shooting on the night of July 31. Candles were ceremoniously laid beneath a memorial tree. The next day, the village of Yellow Springs held a press conference about the event. Thanks were extended to the emergency responders, condolences and prayers were offered to the Schenck family, and counseling sessions were offered to the public. The sessions were in the community center—one session included a canine crisis companion, and another dog was available specifically to people living in the neighborhood where the events unfolded. Some villagers were irate that any sort of sympathies were being offered to the man whom they considered to have started the standoff, but most villagers were shell-shocked by the magnitude of the event and felt that The System had let down a man in the throes of mental illness. Schenck's obituary said that he wished to have a Viking funeral: "Unfortunately, Ohio seems to be short of Viking ship. Some of his ashes will be set afloat later on a model float." He would have been forty-three in October 2013.

A subsequent report commissioned by the Ohio Bureau of Criminal Investigation (BCI) found that many grievous errors occurred during the handling of the situation. The 10,000 hours spent putting together the report revealed that communication was hindered by radio systems that were not compatible; that Schenck's phone had been shot, rendering it useless; and that a Sergeant Spicer from the Greene County Sheriff's Department had disseminated much erroneous information, which, being acted upon, could have resulted in further tragedy. Spicer, an officer for twenty-five years, was charged with five infractions. He was cited for breaking the porch light of a nearby residence in an attempt to provide cover for officers, but the homeowners thought someone was trying to break in and called 911, which gave authorities the impression that Schenck was on the move. Such fears were compounded when Spicer attempted to gain entry to another neighbor's house for a better vantage point, which prompted the second set of neighbors to call 911 about a possible break-in. Spicer was also the officer accused of firing his weapon unnecessarily. After all the dust settled, he was said to have deleted the report of the Schenck event. Ultimately, despite Spicer's confidence in his actions—he "would not change a thing he did that night," he said in his testimony—he was terminated from the sheriff's department.

Overall, however, the report found that officers had acted appropriately. Police protocol is to call a SWAT team when police are dealing with a barricaded person firing shots. The fact that Schenck was intoxicated "does not change the [police's] response protocol," said Major Kirk Keller, a SWAT commander with the sheriff's department, noting that police used significant restraint by not returning fire every time Schenck shot at them. Ohio Attorney General Mike DeWine presented on the BCI's report as well. Ordinarily the report would go straight to prosecutors, but DeWine chose to address the town because it had so many questions about the event. At the press conference, he expressed the need to fix the nation's mental illness infrastructure but said he believed that law enforcement's response was reasonable. "There are lessons we can take from this," he said, "but there is absolutely no evidence that the outcome would have been different." (Those close to Schenck deride the findings of the report as spin that makes the police look like heroes, when in reality, they say, there was absolutely no need for the events to have escalated in the way they did, or for Schenck to have ended up dead.)

In November 2016, Schenck's son, Max Schenck, himself frequently on the police radar for a host of drug crimes and domestic violence, came very close to the same fate that befell his father. Schenck got a ride home from a party with two friends, one of whom was a known cocaine dealer. When they arrived at Schenck's apartment in downtown Yellow Springs, he pulled a gun on his two friends and kept them hostage inside his home, demanding significant amounts of cocaine. The two were held at gunpoint for more than two hours until one of the pair was able to sneak away and call police. Area police and a SWAT team were dispatched to the residence, where the younger Schenck was taken without incident. In addition to the charges he was already facing for assaulting an officer, he faced another fifteen years for the hostage crisis.

To end on a less grisly note, the township has also been host to some crimes that raise an eyebrow in amusement or are almost laughable for their ineptness.[23] In April 1980, a man who received injuries in a recreational basketball game in the town's high school sued the village of Yellow Springs. He and another player got into an altercation after being upset by a ref's call, upon which he was

23. The area has its fair share of ghosts that linger after a tragic death, as if to underscore the injustice that has been done to the township's good name, but there are also a number of light-hearted hauntings that reflect the fact that not every crime is unforgettably inhuman. An amateur folklorist appropriately named Harold Igo collected area ghost lore and published them in a collection, whose tales include "The Case of the Hiccupping Phantom" and "The Story of the Seven Dachshunds." In one story, the "ghosts" in the walls of one house are revealed to be squirrels, while another relates the story of an aunt who had overstayed her welcome and was scared out of a house by the talents of her ventriloquist nephew.

punched so hard in the face that he needed corrective surgery. He sued the man who punched him for $125,000, and the village of Yellow Springs for the same, alleging that the referees employed by the village failed to control players' conduct. The punched man's wife also sued for $25,000 "for loss of her husband's services." It is unclear what came of the dispute.

On March 26, 2009, a man walked into a bank in Yellow Springs and demanded money from a teller. As per protocol, the money was handed over and the subject left without ever brandishing a weapon. The robbery was so low-key that almost nobody else noticed anything amiss in the three minutes the subject was in the building. However, one teller did notice that a tall man in a coat far too heavy for the weather was acting a little strangely, and he pulled the alarm, alerting local authorities to the robbery in progress. The robber, a forty-four-year-old man from Springfield, sealed his fate when he got in his own car after taking the money ("a small amount of cash, but not enough to justify the potential felony charges he will likely face," according to the police chief at the time). The robber was parallel-parked in front of the bank and hit the car behind him three times as he tried to back out. "Watching the offender in bewilderment," a witness reported that the man drove up the road, turned around in a gas station parking lot, and then drove back through the town. A local business's camera caught the vehicle going north and then south down the street, a video from which police were able to identify the plate and trace the vehicle to its registered owner, who matched the description provided by witnesses. The man was soon arrested in his home and said he robbed the bank in order to pay some bills. The same bank (though having a different name)[24] was robbed exactly fifty years before. Another bank was robbed in the 1970s, and in 1996, a man was captured after stealing cash from the teller window of another village bank.

Appendix C contains some lighthearted excerpts from the Yellow Springs News *police report, from August 2015 through the end of 2016.*

---

24. This bank was the sponsor of one of the two basketball teams playing in the game that led to the abovementioned lawsuit.

An Overview of the Township's Celebrity Density, and the Rumor That Lee Harvey Oswald Was in the Area

For a township of its size, Miami Township's celebrity density is surprisingly high. Whether homegrown heroes or Antioch College luminaries, the township's notable residents cross the spectrum of arts, entertainment, and scholarship. Consider the following people, who at one point grew up or lived in Miami Township: renowned children's author Virginia Hamilton; *Twilight Zone* creator Rod Serling; legendary Ohio State University football coach Woody Hayes; Coretta Scott King, who needs no introduction; groundbreaking scientist Stephen J. Gould; Isaac Funk, of Funk and Wagnall's reference work publishers; Mike Kahoe, one of the first Major League Baseball players to wear shin guards; and Irene Bedard, who provided the voice for Pocahontas in the Disney movie *Pocahontas,* and who is also said to have inspired the character's design, as she in fact looks quite a bit like the titular heroine. The township celebrates some of these famous people in an understated way, with a beautiful painting of Virginia Hamilton in the Yellow Springs Library—a life-size portrait depicting the author dressed in a cloak bedecked with characters from her books—but generally leaves these famous people to live their lives in peace.[25]

---

25. The area is also full of people with illustrious minor accomplishments, like Yellow Springs resident Chris Waymire, who took first prize in an online

But the township's two most famous residents are in leagues of their own. One resident can boast of truly international fame and an enduring imprint in the world of comedy, and the other has scrawled a ragged, violent, mysterious mark across pages of U.S. history: superstar comedian Dave Chappelle grew up in Yellow Springs and still resides there, while the village was said to have hosted none other than Lee Harvey Oswald, the man behind the Kennedy assassination (or, depending on who is asked, the fall guy for a larger conspiracy orchestrated by Castro, the Mafia, Russia, vice president Lyndon Johnson, and/or Texas oil barons). In addition to affecting events on a global scale, these two larger-than-life characters have also colored the history and culture of Miami Township.

Gay Talese's profile "Frank Sinatra Has a Cold" describes the far-reaching fallout that occurred when Old Blue Eyes was too sick to perform. Talese writes that the cold threw the routines of his friends, employees, and peripheral acquaintances into disorder as the repercussions of his illness mounted. Dave Chappelle having a mild illness doesn't throw Yellow Springs into a similar level of disarray, but the daily errands of a man of his celebrity nonetheless have repercussions throughout the community.

There are only about two streets in Yellow Springs that aren't residential, and these two streets hold 90 percent of the businesses in town; by default, if Chappelle were to run errands, that's where he would do them. Indeed, Chappelle is often seen in the village, walking down the street and chatting with people, smoking cigarettes or getting a carton of eggs or a cup of coffee, clad in fancy sweatpants and a sleeveless shirt, doing things that demonstrate that celebrities, as *People* magazine loves to put it, are *just like us!* He can sometimes be found holding court next to a coffee shop, perpetually bumming cigarettes to the degree that one person estimated she was owed at least a carton or two. Chappelle drives an understated black sports car and a black SUV, both of which are

grain-marketing contest. Waymire won Penton Media's *Corn and Soybean Digest* MarketMaxx competition in 2007 for his impressive work in the online simulator MarketMaxx, in which farmers use marketing tools to grow their farms. Waymire was presented with a plaque and a write-up in a few local papers, but the major award was one year's worth use of a large combine, a prize valued at $12,000.

FIGURE 19. Celebrity comedian Dave Chappelle, who lives in Miami Township, made national news when he spoke at a meeting of the Yellow Springs Village Council in spring 2017. Chappelle weighed in on the need to repair the relationship between villagers and police.

not too ostentatious; they are hard to notice when parked on the street among other cars, but they will make gearheads stop and take note admiringly. When the sports car was newly purchased, Chappelle could be seen making circles, smoking cigarettes with the car top down, through the town in the middle of the night, like a kid with a new toy. (He also appears in the police report for speeding.)

Chappelle's magnetism is unusual—does he stand out because everyone knows he's a celebrity, or is one of those people who are so naturally magnetic that they are destined to become famous anyway? In late 2016, he signed a deal for more than $60 million to produce four new comedy specials for Netflix. The aura of a man worth that kind of money is palpable, and were Chappelle not a hometown kid (his dad was a professor at Antioch College and a long-standing member of the community), his presence might draw a little more attention. But he lives in Yellow Springs because the townspeople let him do his thing. He has friends in town, knows people by name, and carries on with people in the street or in a shop, a semblance of the life he knew years before. These interactions in turn tend to make people feel good about themselves—people are affected when he nods in their direction or chuckles at their jokes. People get giddy when they talk to him but try to stay casual when doing so—despite one's professed indifference to celebrity culture or fame, being asked for a cigarette or being drawn in with a hello handshake and bro-hug is enough to make someone's day. So affirming is a personal Chappelle salutation that almost everyone is quick to elevate what might otherwise be a glancing acquaintance to a real friendship when describing their relationship to Chappelle. But townspeople can rest assured that he's not just deigning to talk to them—his generosity is such that he's known to give $100 tips when buying a beer at the local bars or eating at area restaurants.

There is a sense of communal pride in his achievements. Chappelle's massive success reflects well on the town he's from. Townspeople are happy that one of their own is so revered, and it is a common topic of conversation in the village when he does something big, like sign that huge Netflix deal or provide incisive commentary on *Saturday Night Live* right after Donald Trump became president. When Chappelle appeared at the 2016 NBA finals, celebrity commentators commented on how muscular he had gotten. This was old hat for people in Yellow Spring, as he is typically wearing a shirt free of sleeves, and people have been able to observe his muscular development for years (if not train him themselves, as one of his trainers lives in town). He'll occasionally mention Yellow Springs in an interview, which townspeople are happy to post en masse on their Facebook walls. It was literally international news when he spoke at a Yellow Springs Village Council Meeting about the local police department's arguably heavy-handed tactics over the previous few years.

Every year, Chappelle throws one of the area's premier parties, at which he is MC and DJ and introduces well-known performers in order to raise money for a nonprofit cause. Ticket prices have increased every year; the 2016 party was $75 per person and included attendees like Bradley Cooper, Naomi Campbell, and Talib Kweli, who, in addition to being in Yellow Springs, posted items on social media showing them en route to the small Ohio hamlet like it was the happening place to be. For two nights in October, music could be heard from across the rolling farmlands outside the village, with blue and purple lights bouncing around the walls of the restored barn hosting the extravagant party. It's unusual to have a celebrity in your midst, but it's a fun quirk that the township has worked into its tapestry.

FIGURE 20. Kennedy's assassin and alleged patsy, Lee Harvey Oswald, was said to have possibly attended Antioch College in the early 1960s. Photo of Antioch courtesy of Antioch College. Oswald mug shot courtesy of the Dallas Police Department.

The other most famous person said to have set foot in the township is not a movie star, was not known to be particularly generous, and committed an act of such infamy that previous acquaintances disavowed knowing him completely: Lee Harvey Oswald.

To be fair, the lofty claim that Oswald was in the township is tenuous at best, based mostly on rumor or misheard information. It was claimed he was enrolled at Antioch College in the 1960s, which at the time was a hotbed of left-wing activism and frequently on the government's radar. So it makes sense that the country's foremost Russian émigré would be linked to such an institution in an attempt to discredit both. The government kept files on students and student groups associated with the college, and when it turned out that an Antioch grad named Ruth Paine was closely connected to Oswald, his name was quickly linked to the college as well.

Ruth Paine graduated Antioch in 1955 and eventually moved to Irving, Texas, with her husband and their children. There she befriended Marina Oswald, Lee Harvey's wife, who had come to the United States with Oswald after his stint in Russia. Paine, who spoke Russian, met Marina through a friend. When Oswald moved around Texas looking for work, Marina and their two children would stay with Paine. In October 1963, Oswald got a job filling orders at the Texas School Book Depository. On November 21, 1963, he came to retrieve some of his belongings from Paine's garage, including the Carcano Model 91/38 carbine rifle he would use to kill Kennedy the next day, shooting him from the sixth floor of the depository.

Paine was promptly questioned by the FBI after the assassination, and she later testified at the Warren Commission, the official government agency that conducted the inquiry into Kennedy's death. During her testimony, she discussed her time at Antioch and admitted having read Marx and Engels's *The Communist Manifesto* in a class. She said she had no interest in it beyond the class, nor did she have any interest in Marx's *Das Kapital*. "I have seen the size of the book, and I certainly would not want to read it," she told the commission.

Paine also discovered by accident that Oswald had attempted to assassinate a Texas gubernatorial candidate named General Edwin Walker, who was essentially uninjured in the attack. (The attempt on Walker's life was, of course, news at the time, but police had no leads on a suspect.) But Paine was not considered to have any sort of involvement with Oswald's nefarious deeds and was able to live a fairly normal life after the assassination. She eventually got her master's degree and became a school psychologist. The home where the rifle was held was purchased by the city of Irving, Texas, and turned into a museum.

The rumors connecting Oswald and Paine to the area started a few weeks after the assassination. The *Columbus Dispatch* wrote an article about the Paine-Antioch connection, noting that Paine had learned Russian from Marina Oswald, that she considered learning the Russian language a hobby, and that she was a Quaker and a pacifist. The addresses of Paine's parents and family, who lived in Columbus, were published in their entirety in the article. The same article reported that Antioch students were among those involved in a demonstration by the Fair Play for Cuba Committee in front of the statehouse in Columbus. In November 1963, a Columbus police officer received information from an anonymous source that Lee Harvey Oswald had attempted to enroll at Antioch in 1957 but was not accepted because he couldn't prove he graduated high school.

A Cincinnati FBI agent issued a report in early 1964 suggesting that Oswald was receiving money orders through a bank in Yellow Springs. But this allegation has "completely run out and has proven to have no basis in fact," and the report was not disseminated outside the office. In fact, a now-declassified document mentions how the agents associated with the rumor were chastised: "Personnel of the Cincinnati Office who were responsible for the poor wording in the report [about] the Oswald case have been issued sharp error slips . . . and have been issued emphatic admonitions."

However, it is possible that the government distorted "official" accounts of Oswald's whereabouts, as many believe he was a CIA operative who only *appeared* to be a pro-Castro agitator. The story goes that when the government orchestrated Kennedy's assassination, they had the perfect person to blame it on, Oswald, because he was already known as a vocal Communist who had defected to Russia.

Following this logic, some say, Oswald's connection with Ruth Paine, who also happened to speak Russian, likely means that she too was a CIA operative. And taking this further, if Oswald and Paine were both CIA operatives with connections to Antioch, then it's possible that Antioch was—or still is—connected to the CIA.

The story of Antioch College itself is a whirlwind.[26] Founded as a religious-oriented institution in May 1852, it was one of the first coed institutions of higher learning and was designed to be a progressive institution from the get-go. Horace Mann, the first president of the college, said that he would "never consent to be connected with an institution from which any person of requisite qualifications would be excluded on grounds of color, sex, physical deformity, or anything from which such person was not morally responsible." Such a legacy continued following the Civil War and into the twentieth century. Many elderly residents of color cite the manifest seriousness of the commitment to social justice and equity held by Antioch staff. One African American woman received paid training from the college's president to go to a trade school and was then hired at the college, an arrangement essentially unheard of at the time. By the 1960s, the culture of forward-thinking activism melded with the tune in/turn on/drop out ethos of the hippies, and for the next few decades, Antioch's reputation diminished as more "radical" educational philosophies were said by some of the old guard to take precedence over much actual learning (though many repudiate the notion that left-

26. For more on when and how the university (vs. the college) came into being, see https://www.antioch.edu/why-au/au-history/ and http://www.daytoncitypaper.com/im-antioch/.

ist politics had sunk the school and attribute the difficulties more to high staff turnover and sloppy financial management). While still a historically respected institution, attendance slowly dwindled. The college had a peak of 2,000 students in the 1950s; by the late 1990s, there were only a few hundred. For an unaccredited, tuition-funded school with a relatively small endowment, the financial viability of the institution was precarious to the degree that members of staff took "payless paydays," with promises from the college that the delayed funds would somehow be paid to them later. In the early 2000s, when the college was in a "state of preemergency," the college voted to overhaul the school's approach to education, "dramatically altering a system that, educationally [at least], wasn't working." The new approach didn't do much to increase the number of incoming students, nor did a $5 million accounting error that showed the school had even less money that it realized.

It wasn't just dwindling attendance that affected the prominence of the school but also some restructuring that led to internal competition. In addition to maintaining Antioch College, Antioch University opened thirty campuses across the country in the 1970s. (Four remain as of late 2017.) These campuses are geared toward commuting and adult learners, including one on the other side of Yellow Springs (Antioch University Midwest). The universities have proven to be monetarily viable institutions (although they are private, nonprofit, 503[3][c] entities), and the college and the universities were merged under the umbrella of Antioch University. As time went by, the less viable Antioch College increasingly appeared to be a burden. According to one observer, "The notion of the College being central to the university [became] primarily a social conceit—and one which the other branches of the university eventually learned they could ignore."

Eventually, the board of the Antioch University network removed what they called an unsuccessful president at Antioch College, furthering the rift between the college and the universities. Antioch College's finances became so perilously low that the Antioch University board chose to close the college at the end of the 2008 school year: the college was entirely shut down in favor of the satellite universities.

Outcry against the decision from college alumni and supporters was enormous, and through their College Revival Fund they eventually raised enough money (more than $18 million) to reopen the college. In the interim, while the school was closed, former staff formed Nonstop Antioch, a group that continued to teach in buildings in and around Yellow Springs. Classes were conducted in businesses, churches, and homes and drew at least twenty full-time college students and almost sixty part-time students from the school and the community. So concerted was the Nonstop effort that the College Revival Fund earmarked $1 million from its pledged donations to go toward the activities of Nonstop Antioch. "Nonstop had an enormous symbolic importance," said one Nonstop student. "Nationally, we were a beacon of resistance in the struggle against the corporatization of higher education. We showed that a college is not about resources and buildings. It's about the faculty, students and the community." (Antioch University's lawyers sent a letter to the seventeen staff members involved in Nonstop, threatening legal action for inappropriate use of the Antioch name unless the staff wrote letters of assurance saying they would dispense with the term "Antioch" in their activities.[27] The name was changed to the Nonstop Liberal Arts Institute.)

After a few years of walking a tense financial tightrope, followed by a grueling year in which the decision to close the college was finally made, and then the whirlwind few years of fund-raising and the activities of Nonstop, the denouement was that Antioch College would reopen as an independent institution of higher learning, entirely free from the control of its offshoot-turned-overlord, Antioch University. The college reopened in time to welcome the freshman class of 2012, drawing new students thanks in part to its generous full-ride tuition scholarships to all incoming students for the following four years.

Reopening the college was like starting over, so the board of trustees at the new college did not rehire any of the Nonstop staff back as faculty members, or many other people who had previously worked at the college (though some former faculty were rehired in key administrative positions). Many Nonstop support-

---

27. According to an attorney representing Antioch University, unauthorized used "is likely to deceive the public with respect to Antioch's trademarks and associated services and dilute the distinctiveness of the well-known Antioch marks and logos. The unauthorized use of Antioch's valuable trademarks will cause confusion and improperly benefit you to the detriment of Antioch."

ers were shocked at this betrayal, but at least the college was back on its feet.

Attendance at Antioch College is still low—2016's incoming class was only forty-four students—but the college maintains its reputation for activism and progressive education, and the college was granted accreditation by the Higher Learning Commission in 2016. However, some people are wary of the college's resurrection. Some put forth the idea that the reopening of the college was not necessarily due to the munificence of its former students but the calculated machinations of a sinister cabal promoting New World Order–style global domination. Columbus journalist, lawyer, and recent County Prosecutor candidate Bob Fitrakis outlined the eyebrow-raising connections of the new Antioch's new board and staff.

In addition to past Antioch professors who had worked for government security agencies, Fitrakis wrote that a few former members of Antioch University's board of trustees have connections to corporations that provide defense technology solutions to the Department of Homeland Security, the Department of Defense, and other intelligence agencies.[28] In other words, the college's vaunted left-wing tradition had been taken over by businesses that developed war technology. One higher-education blogger called the allegations "a nearly-impenetrable and logic-free collection of conspiracy theories" and made sure to stress numerous times that the closing of the College could be blamed squarely on the $5 million accounting error,[29] but Fitrakis maintained that the people on the board of Antioch University warrant some scrutiny, as do the reasons they closed it. For example, Bruce P. Bedford, appointed to the board of the now-defunct GlobeSecNine, a company involved with specialized forces and military operations solu-

28. See https://freepress.org/article/did-us-intelligence-assets-kill-antioch-college.

29. This blogger wrote a post roundly decrying Fitrakis's allegations but was in turn lambasted for not being willing to believe something fishy might be going on. He seemed to have taken the accusations personally: "It is disingenuous to call someone's critical thinking into question because they dismiss an unsupported theory out of hand in favor of one that is supported," he wrote. ". . . When you believe a crazy conspiracy theory instead of simple accounting facts, when you're not bravely questioning the status quo of joining the camps of Galileo and other status-quo-questioners throughout history, you're simply off the deep end, and Galileo wouldn't be pleased."

tions. GlobeSecNine had a "strategic alliance" with The Scowcroft Group, a firm headed by Brent Scowcroft, former National Security Advisor to presidents George H. W. Bush and Gerald Ford. Lawrence Stone, who vociferously advocated for Antioch's closing, is former CFO (2004–10) of Metron, Inc., which works with naval and space defense agencies and lists as a client CACI International Inc., the company that provided interrogators to Abu Ghraib. Michael Alexander, a trustee whose name was removed from all public lists of trustees, founded AveStar Capital, which did business with NASA and the Defense Department. AveStar was sold to the Titan Corporation, which in 2005 paid the largest fine in history ($28 million) for bribery and tax fraud under the rules of the Corrupt Foreign Practices Act. The Titan Corporation was in turn sold to L-3 Communications, which develops defense technologies; 80 percent of its 10,000 employees have security clearances.

While Fitrakis doesn't make any outright allegations, he does say that their timing on the board was suspicious: the members of the board, at the behest of the CIA, killed Antioch college, which, the members believed, had outlived its usefulness as an intelligence/ infiltration asset. Moreover, the Antioch board hired a public relations firm to negotiate its closing, and this firm, SimpsonScarborough, was headed by Christopher Simpson, a former right-wing journalist who worked for a paper owned by the Reverend Sun Myung Moon, the founder of the Moonie cult and a member of the Korean CIA (the latter association according to the American CIA). Simpson himself used to be press secretary for Strom Thurmond. Fitrakis also says that one shouldn't fail to notice the college's proximity to Wright-Patterson Air Force Base[30] or The Ohio State University, the latter of whom works very closely with the "CIA's favorite nonprofit Battelle," a secretive research company whose campus is located right next to the university.

However, Antioch may not be a CIA front *in toto*; it may just have been infiltrated. "If the CIA or U.S. intelligence services were involved in the subversion of America's most pro-peace college, it wouldn't be the first time that the progressive college campuses

---

30. Wright-Patterson is held by many to be the *real* Area 51, the place they took the debris from the Roswell crash to study in secret laboratories many stories underground. High-tech flight technology that has been developed at the base is said to be based on alien technology.

have been infiltrated," writes Fitrakis. "The CIA subverted the National Student Association in the late 50s and early 60s. The agency also has been accused of subverting everything from fraternities to Fulbright scholars to Peace Corps workers."

Either way, the Oswald connection, to say nothing of the saga of Antioch College/University itself, is an interesting historical note, exactly the kind of thing that makes a book about Miami Township so interesting and valuable.

CHAPTER 8

The Fiscal Officer's Report

By this point, all that was left of the September 9 meeting of the Miami Township Board of Trustees were a few final odds and ends, such as presentation of the Fiscal Officer's Report and the Zoning Inspector's Report, which happens only at the first meeting of each month.

Margaret Silliman has been the township's fiscal officer since 2000. The township's budget is just under $1 million per year, and it is Silliman's job to manage the township's budget and keep its records, from recording the minutes at meetings to appropriating funds to writing all payroll checks. The office is accorded many other duties as well: in the absence of a fire department, for example, the fiscal officer is the official representative to the state fire marshal outside the incorporated areas of the township. Just like the trustees, fiscal officers have their own *Ohio Township Sourcebook,* with straightforward explanations of Ohio Code and the whats and hows of what fiscal officers can actually do. Indeed, the work done by the fiscal officer keeps the official township steamroller going, practically, financially, and methodologically.

Two items were listed under the Fiscal Officer's Report section of the September 9 agenda. The items were two resolutions, relatively small-scale procedural motions that nonetheless needed official approval to be implemented. Resolution 2015-14 was an

FIGURE 21. Miami Township fiscal officer Margaret Silliman. Photo courtesy of the *Yellow Springs News.*

Amendment of Permanent Appropriations that earmarked money for use across many departments (including allocating more money for the cemetery's electric bill), while Resolution 2015-15 requested a transfer of $10,000 from the township's general fund to its cemetery fund in order to pay for some upkeep and the exploration with ground-penetrating radar.

Monies in the general fund come from property taxes and a local government fund run by the state, which apportions money to help entities like townships conduct their business. The general fund used to be funded in part by estate taxes, but the Ohio legislature repealed estate tax entirely for anyone who died on or after January 1, 2013. Money for the fire department comes in part from levies passed specifically to fund the fire department, while road maintenance in part comes from taxes on gasoline; thus, money in those funds cannot be used for anything other than the utility they are designated to finance.

But funds from the general fund can be moved around to pay for bills in any department the township needs—hence the resolution to transfer some money to the cemetery. In some respects, Silliman said, the cemetery was foisted onto the township, creating an expense that might not have otherwise been there. Money coming into the cemetery "depends on people dying" and their relatives paying for plots, a revenue stream that no trustee or financial officer would encourage, even if it was financially beneficial.

The financial resolutions that had to be passed at the meeting on September 9 were fairly routine: some general moving around of money that happens not infrequently at trustee meetings. After following the familiar and rapid-fire Roberts Rules–influenced procedure, the resolutions were adopted by the trustees.[31] Silliman also noted that insurance providers had changed and that she would be going to a sort of conference of her own, a public budget hearing hosted by the county auditor. She extended her invitation to the other trustees, none of whom jumped at the chance to go with her.

No matter how routine, each of the township's financial transactions is tracked by the state. The township uses accounting software that is tied into the offices of state auditors, and any expenditures that differ from the financial plan submitted at the beginning of each year have to be passed by official trustee resolution. The State of Ohio audits a township's books every two years, both because they must do so in the interest of transparency and possibly because there are no specific qualifications to become a township fiscal officer aside from being of age and a citizen of the township and of the United States. Silliman met these qualifications, and her viability for fiscal officer was bolstered by her eight years of experience as the clerk of the Yellow Springs Village Council and her abiding interest in helping people. She said she is fascinated by the concerns and philosophies that make people tick, both of which are readily observed in her role as a public servant.

Silliman grew up in Cincinnati, went to college at Ohio University, and moved to Yellow Springs in 1979 as a young mother. Her

---

31. "Whereas it is the intent of the Miami Township trustees to distribute funds appropriately and fiscally responsibly; and whereas it is the desire of the trustees to support the expenses of the Glen Forest Cemetery. Now therefore be it resolved that the MTTT authorize the fiscal officer to transfer $10,000 from the General Fund to 2042 Glen Forest Cemetery."

husband was from nearby Enon, which Silliman said is "none" spelled backward and makes for a pretty good approximation of what's going on in that town. She set down roots in Yellow Springs and raised a son and a daughter in the village. Like many other people in the area, she took a number of part-time jobs in order to make ends meet, at one point working in a few restaurants and at the *Yellow Springs News*. In 1990, she was asked to be clerk of council for the Yellow Springs Village Council, a position that at the time was dedicated exclusively to taking the minutes of the meeting. She had no formal training in parliamentary procedure but was able to pick up the duties quickly. (While Silliman's position as clerk was never more than part-time, the council now has a full-time clerk with an assistant, owing to things going "cray-cray" ["You can quote me on that," said Silliman] in the council over some contentious local issues. Village council meetings now regularly run four hours or more, and Silliman holds a different position; see below.)

Silliman was already "naturally interested" in small-town politics and became "hooked on village government" as she spent more time as clerk. But she noticed that many of the people who were irate about how their government had failed them didn't actually know how government processes officially worked. "People come riding in on emotion rather than fact," she said, and as she grew more comfortable in her role as a functionary, she began to appreciate her role as someone who could be a "reliable source of information" for the villagers about how village government works. Having a better understanding of the process might help people become more interested in participating in governmental affairs, again an opportunity Silliman felt was engaging and important.

She took the minutes of council meetings for almost eight years before taking a break from thinking and writing in officialese. However, when Silliman's township fiscal officer predecessor, Marsha Adams Hickman, left after one term, a few people at the township asked Silliman to consider becoming the township's clerk, because she had experience at the village council and was a well-known person-about-town, as she was a bartender at a local restaurant. After running and winning the 2000 election, Silliman found herself Miami Township's financial officer. She quickly saw that she and the other trustees had a good personal and professional relationship. She already knew Spracklen, having met him while campaigning and eventually living in a house on a property he owned, and had known Mark Crockett and his wife, Gail Zimmerman, since she moved to Yellow Springs, in fact spending her first New Year's Eve in the village at their house.

Though she previously only took minutes at the village council meetings, Silliman's new role required her to execute complex bookkeeping and payroll maneuvers, such as paying into a pension fund for employees and filing withheld federal taxes the day a paycheck is issued. However, taking minutes is still a big part of her duties as fiscal officer, and one that she does dutifully. Though she is only required to attend four meetings per year and can take minutes after the fact from the video that's taken of every meeting, she finds its easier just to attend the meetings when they happen: she knows where she'll be the first and third Monday evenings of each month and that taking minutes while physically there is less tedious than making time to watch a video of a meeting at another time that week.

While it's rare that she goes back and looks at the minutes from past meetings—"I don't want to characterize the meetings as undignified, but not a lot happens"—preserving arguments for posterity when they do happen is important for the township's historical record. Silliman truly got to live out this responsibility at the meeting on September 9 and at the follow-up meeting two weeks later, when she recorded everything everyone said in their arguments for and against the Glen House Inn. Ordinarily she is able to record an abridged version of what is said at the meetings—"I don't write every word of a discussion about lawnmowers," she said, as in-depth discussions of lawnmowers are known to take place—but the Glen House Inn arguments were recorded verbatim based on the caliber of the dispute, something she had never had to do before. "Everyone wanted to be heard, so I had to fulfill that wish," she said.

Though the Glen House Inn B&B controversy was easily the most contentious issue that has faced the township in recent memory, the trustees were able to see the dispute through with relative unanimity, a sign of the amiable professionalism characteristic of the township's current administration. "I've acquired a huge amount of love and respect for the people that work" in the township, Silliman said, especially the volunteers at MTFR. "A lot of people don't realize that many of the people working to save your life are volunteers," she said of the firefighters. "They know their shit, and it's really cool to feel connected to that." Moreover, the trustees are in agreement that the rural character of the township should be maintained, lest it end up like nearby Beavercreek, another early settlement in southwestern Ohio that went the way of many previously pristine environments. "Back in the day, Beavercreek was where beavers flopped in creeks. Now it's almost all development," she said.

But life in the township offices wasn't always that easy. In fact, it wasn't that easy in the administration preceding Silliman's arrival. Her immediate predecessor was Marsha Adams Hickman, and one of the most crucial duties Silliman undertook upon taking office was to try to sort out (and correct) Hickman's slipshod accounting practices.

Hickman was elected to the office in the 1995 elections, immediately succeeding her mother as township clerk. Her mother was a clerk at the local bank and a well-liked woman around town, so Marsha's campaign signs said "Elect Marsha ADAMS Hickman," in an effort to put forth the idea that the same person was running, or at least to remind voters of the connection. Come Election Day, she breezily beat her opponent, "even though Hickman did not campaign aggressively and was the only candidate who did not attend the Candidate Forum," according to the *Yellow Springs News*. Hickman's lack of presence in the election foreshadowed the distance with which she would approach her tenure as township clerk, and her comments to the *News* upon being elected would seem especially ironic a few years hence. "The most important role of a township clerk involves stewardship of the people's money," she said, "done honestly and with accuracy and effectiveness."

While Hickman started her job on the right foot, a problematic pattern soon emerged. Minutes from one meeting in 1999 noted that Hickman apologized and vowed to do better in response to a reprimand for slacking on her duties. It wasn't the first or last time that her work habits had been criticized by the rest of the township government. "Oh boy, my friend Marsha Hickman . . . ," Mucher said with a shake of the head when asked about her. But the true extent of Hickman's negligence didn't make itself known until the summer of 2000.

Hickman moved out of Yellow Springs in March 2000, shortly after her term ended, though by all accounts she had checked out many months before that. Less than a month later, trustees asked the State Auditor's office for help after Mucher came across a number of accounting errors in books for the years 1998 and 1999. Mucher also found $215,000 in undeposited checks in township offices and also overdraft notices from a bank, which came from over $35,000 in bounced checks. Moreover, meetings minutes had not been kept since the meeting of September 20, 1999. Part of the reason for the gross mismanagement was said to come from the fact that the township was transitioning from an oversized paper ledger to an automated accounting computer program. Hickman had never gotten comfortable with the computer system, a deficiency that compounded her lack of preparedness for the job, "either by disposition, intention, or ability." "I'm not surprised," Mucher said at the time the errors were discovered. "We anticipated a difficult time with the records."

But even Mucher must have been surprised at the extent of the negligence. Soon after the work began, the auditor's office couldn't proceed with getting everything in order due to a significant amount of missing records, including missing W-2s, payroll documents, bank statements, and purchase orders. "The missing documents do not mean that the township is missing funds, only paperwork," Mucher clarified at a meeting. The auditors stopped their work until such documents could be retrieved. Copies of many documents were on file with Greene County and other agencies and banks, which the township had to track down in order to finish the work. A headline in the *Yellow Springs News* laid out the situation bluntly: "State Auditor Finds Township Books Are Unauditable," it read.

The trustees eventually decided to cancel the audit. Mucher said they had already spent $4,000 getting everything in order to be audited, and reconstructing and retrieving the lost documents would cost just as much. Doing this would be a waste of taxpayer money, he said. The audit was for the township's own purposes and not mandated by the state, so trustees decided to just tough it out, doing their best to organize material that was not filed "in a manner that is easily retrievable." It would be possible to hold Hickman legally responsible for the financial headaches she created, including being "fined for recovery," which means that the township is fined by the state if they have to reconstruct the official township paper trail. The township hired a bookkeeping firm familiar with township operations to explore the issue further, and the fine was lifted when the firm was able to satisfactorily produce the information requested by the state.

Township trustees have the power to remove a financial officer, a lengthy process that was made only slightly easier in recent years by the state court system. But no proceedings were ever brought against Hickman, nor were any fines levied. In fact, Mucher said he never heard from Hickman after she left town, an outcome that didn't engender any satisfying legal comeuppance but was nonetheless probably best for everyone.

Mucher expressed some surprise that the fiscal officer position would be taken for granted. Clerks often run unopposed, meaning that once somebody is in office, it's unlikely they will face much competition in the foreseeable future. It's "a great job, and you practically have it for life," Mucher said. But despite the promise of an enduring job with insurance, the draw was not enough for Hickman, who unfortunately has to live with the checkered legacy she sketched out for herself in the annals of township history. Silliman's tenure has been far more productive, as aside from a few accidental accounting snafus, the township government has been free of much conflict or scolding by the state.

But not entirely free: the township was fined for recovery in 2013 when state auditors found $11,624 worth of problems with their books. Some of that money—$5,849—was on the books but not in the township's bank accounts, while the rest was money overpaid to the trustees and the fiscal officer. Silliman was truly perplexed by the disparity and pored over the books to find out what it was. "It's not that there's money missing per se," she said at the time. "There's got to be a bookkeeping error in there." There did prove to be an error in record keeping, which solved the matter of the $5,849.

Although it may seem damning that the remaining $5,775 went into the accounts of township officials, that error could be explained by the sliding scale of trustee wages. Trustees are paid a certain amount according to the township's budget, and in 2008 to 2009, the township's budget was over $1.5 million, which pushed their pay grade to the next level. Sanctioned by state auditors, Silliman had adjusted their paychecks to account for the raise but then forgot to lower them to the previous level when the township's budget shrank to below $1.5 million a year later. Silliman and the trustees were ordered to pay the money back but were not considered guilty of anything worse than on-the-job mistakes.

"Watch the cash, watch the law," a state auditor warned, or "you're going to owe the taxpayers some money."[32]

Chastened by the oversight and the subsequent fine for recovery, Silliman pays much closer attention to every line item and every dollar spent. It's not just the duty to the township that she has to consider but the luck of finding a job that keeps her engaged. "I couldn't do a job where I sat at a desk isolated by a computer screen and with no human interactions," she said, shuddering as she said this. Not only is Silliman able to indulge her interest in helping resident solve the problems they face, but she is able to take advantage of luxuries not many jobs afford, such as decent health insurance and the ability to choose her own hours. All in all, the job is not something Silliman takes for granted.

---

32. As evidenced by the above difficulties, mild scandals occasionally crop up in every stratum of government. Another interesting example is a problem faced by the Yellow Springs Village Council in May 1981. A state auditor found that the village had illegally spent more than $7,000 on coffee and lunches for its employees. The initial scandal was christened "Coffeegate," as questionable coffee expenses comprised 90 percent of the disputed funds. The rest of the money went to lunches and was thus referred to as "Lunchgate." The village had stopped its coffee-buying practices in February of the previous year but passed a resolution allowing for the buying of lunches when "necessary in the service of public interest." Meeting for lunch was one of the best ways to "improve [the village's] relations with the business sector," said one official, noting that the officials involved would definitely not be paying anything back. The state auditor eventually offered to drop the matter if the village simply changed its practices. "Our main concern is that this practice be stopped," said an auditor at the time. "If the village will stop it, our objective will be realized. We see no need to get into a legal battle about it."

A state official did admit that the state was looking for a test case to bring before the Supreme Court, but since Coffeegate was nowhere near as egregious as the practices of some towns in which "public officials go to lunch every day on the public," the state wouldn't be pursuing the matter any further.

Though the Ohio legislature is considering adopting more regulations and qualifications for the office of fiscal officer, right now the job lets officers rely on their wiles and experience to get the job done. "I could go to conferences and get various certifications, but I'm content in the position I'm in and don't need any titles next to my name," Silliman said. Thanks to her more than sixteen years of expertise (plus eight if counting her time at the village council), the township has run smoothly and accurately, and without any further need for a closer look by the state.

CHAPTER 9

The Zoning Inspector's Report

Following Silliman's presentation at the meeting on September 9 was the zoning inspector's report, which was to be delivered by township zoning inspector Richard Zopf. Zopf had had a rough go of it for the duration of the evening, as he was the recipient of many unfettered political and personal criticisms from people on both sides of the Glen House Inn B&B issue. He sat up at the table in front of the room in the MTFR building, dignified by his seat at the table but as weary as anyone would be after such a volley of attacks.

"I think I've taken up a chunk of your meeting tonight," Zopf said when it was his time to present.

A significant amount of his own time had recently been dedicated to wrestling with the B&B issue, he said, and not just at that evening's meeting. Members of the CCC had also pleaded their case against the inn at the recent zoning board meeting, which Zopf is also part of, meaning that Zopf had been engaged with the dispute in two separate meetings, on the phone when people called to chew him out for not acting fast enough, and on-site whenever he was called to check out a grievance against the inn or to be shown that a previous grievance was now up to code.

Despite his slightly frazzled bearing, he continued with his report, as he did have to some business to present separate from the B&B controversy.

He said he had recently attended a meeting with the county zoning inspector, the county zoning administrator, and a regional planning group. They talked about a lot of things, he said, though none were particularly relevant to what was happening at the meeting. Zopf had issued one permit since they last met and gave an update on some people who were living in a structure that was never intended to be a home. "They are working with me on that to square it away," he said.

True to his word, Zopf's report didn't go longer than two minutes, though, coupled with the arguments from earlier that evening, one could make the case that issues pertinent to township zoning ran well over an hour and did in fact take up a large portion of the meeting.

But they weren't quite done with the B&B yet. Capping off Zopf's section of the evening's meeting was the finalizing of plans to visit the Glen House Inn on September 14. Hayden said she could draft a complaint that would be ready to file against the inn as soon as early October, and, until then, she reiterated that she would draft a Formal Notice of Violation letter to serve the Owens with, the "fill in the blank" letter that Owen said proved the township was prejudiced against the inn from the start, as it showed they came in with an agenda instead of checking things out for themselves first. Hayden said would visit the inn with the rest of the county officials on September 14, at which time she said she would deliver the violation letter herself. It would be easier to serve the Owens at this meeting than trying to track them down out of state, she said, which, in her experience, can take weeks.

(If the Owens were interested in pointing out where the township and county appeared to collude against them, it was here they felt they had the most solid evidence that it was true. As it turned out, the Owens *were* interested in pointing out this apparent collusion, and Erik let everyone know at the September 21 meeting that there was what amounted to almost conspiracy at the meeting two weeks before.)

All in all, though, despite the high tension surrounding the issue, the B&B dispute was at that point able to be discussed in a more relaxed manner, as all of the incensed neighbors had left and township officials were able to reflect a little more loosely on how to handle the affair.

Dale Amstutz was there for reasons both personal and professional, as he sat on the township's Zoning Commission and was curious about the zoning issues surrounding the Glen House Inn. He spoke with the trustees at length about the situation, offering his informed opinion on zoning matters and trying to weigh things from all sides. Mark Crockett spoke next. "The thing about process," he began in his characteristically drawn-out delivery, "is that it's evolved to protect individuals." Trustees are not able to pronounce judgment of guilty or not guilty on citizens, he said, and began listing off the other boards and courts that the state has in place to suss out someone's guilt. The other people at the table seemed eager to avoid what was shaping up to be a theory-heavy discussion, and the conversation was subtly brought around to the topic at hand in order to keep the meeting moving forward.

Miami Township zoning inspector Richard Zopf has a frizzy white beard and keeps his considerably long legs clad in tiny, home-hemmed shorts and mid-calf hiking boots for most of the year. He looks not unlike the leader of some kind of expedition into the bush, not far a cry from his current job description, which sometimes has him inspecting the wilder edges of someone's property.

So what does the zoning inspector do? Different areas of the township are zoned according to their use. An area can be zoned residential, commercial, industrial, or agricultural (with further distinctions within these categories); the uses are self-explanatory. There are different rules and regulations regarding permissible building and development for each of these, and, since 1947, state law grants individual Ohio townships the freedom to determine the acceptable sizes and uses of buildings built on each zone in the township, "in the interest of public safety," and it is up to the zoning inspector to make sure that the respective zoning ordinances are being followed. In most cases, a property owner will meet with the zoning inspector before building. They'll go over the rules, and if the plans seem to square with what the township zoning code permits, the inspector will issue a permit giving the property owner the go-ahead to complete the project.

Of course, there are complex rules for what can be built, and why and how, and who has to sign off on it depending on the intended use of the prospective building. Sometimes township zoning inspectors have complete oversight over a project while sometimes a project requires permission from different combinations of departments from all strata of state government. In the case of the Glen House Inn, the number of guests allowed at the B&B was determined by township code, the septic system overseen by Greene County, and the sprinkler systems of a commercial enterprise overseen by the state fire marshal. In order to operate the B&B as the Owens intended, they would have had to get the appropriate certificate from these (and other) agencies. The confusion over who gives what permission was one of the centerpieces of the Owens' defense. For the most part, though, when someone in the township wants to build a structure on his or her property, those inspections do not typically balloon in scope, or even take longer than a quick survey of the site and plans.

Townships also determine the appropriate size of signs, acceptable use of trailers on properties, and other such considerations, any of which can lead to a dispute. "Because the zoning enforcement officer is responsible for approving or denying zoning permits, residents may be passionate about the zoning permit process and may feel that it is an invasion of their property rights," says one zoning inspector website.[33] Often, the zoning inspector bears the brunt of a homeowner's ire, as was the case with the Glen House Inn, when Zopf and Deb Leopold, the director of the GCCHD, competed to be the face of needless government meddling.

Most of the calls Zopf gets about zoning questions come from appraisers who are evaluating a piece of property and want to get an idea of how it can be used (and thus marketed) to prospective buyers. "Rarely does a homeowner call me up and ask me what their property is zoned," he said. "They either seem to know or it doesn't make any difference to them." When residents do have a question, however, it tends to be from property owners who want to build a new building or an accessory structure on the property, such as a shed or garage, or modify one already there. Modifications on a structure that don't expand its footprint—such as removing a room—don't require a zoning permit, nor does demolition, such as tearing down a garage.

Interestingly, the state is very clear about township officials not having any say over what happens on a property zoned agricul-

---

33. See https://ohioline.osu.edu/factsheet/CDFS-1281.

tural, perhaps a reflection of the significant role that farmers play in Ohio's economy. In almost all cases, building a new structure for agricultural purposes requires no permit at all.[34] If a farmer wants to put up a building to house a tractor or to store grain, he or she could do this, no questions asked.[35] In fact, citizens can do pretty much anything they want if it is for agricultural purposes, such as growing corn on a property zoned industrial. Recall that Erik Owen threatened to turn his barn into a winery, a pursuit that was considered agricultural and may have allowed him to get away with much more than he was with a B&B in an area zoned residential.

Though Zopf is said to sometimes "speak in riddles" about the already riddle-like official township rules, he is an experienced zoner and a hardy civil servant. A look at his life outside zoning shows that his choice to take on the embattled duties of the zoning inspector fifteen years before comes not from a love of ruthlessly enforcing code but from a sense of responsibility he feels to the community.

Zopf came to the township around fifty years ago and has been active in different community organizations since then. He had served as a Boy Scout troop leader and is a prominent member of the local chapter of the Independent Order of Odd Fellows, one of those old-school social clubs with a charitable focus. One winter, the local chapter got in touch with the Yellow Springs Senior Center and asked whom they might be able to help. The senior center directed Zopf and his fellow Odd Fellows to the homes of twelve seniors, who, after a serious snowstorm, found their driveways and sidewalks shoveled in the night. "I'm just struck dumb," said one resident whose driveway was shoveled. "It's amazing. Like a fairy came in the night." Zopf was modest about the service, insisting that he simply loves shoveling and as a boy was disappointed that he lived on a road that didn't have sidewalks

---

34. The rules aren't quite as lax as they may seem: you don't need a building or zoning permit to build an agricultural building, but you *do* need a permit if you're putting in plumbing or electricity in that building; the permit is given by the county and requires an agricultural exemption granted by the township. Zopf said it makes sense to just go get the exemption when you start construction, as it's cheap and easy to do and will save some hassle down the road.

35. However, using this building for anything but agriculture is verboten. You can't park a car in there alongside your tractor, Zopf said, or build a shed and call your lawnmower agricultural.

that needed to be shoveled.[36] Zopf's wife was a long-serving member of the Yellow Springs School District Board of Education, and in the *Yellow Springs News'* annual feature of reader-submitted "Acts of Kindness," the president of the Yellow Springs Chamber of Commerce and the village council wrote to personally thank Zopf and another Odd Fellow for their contributions to the 2015 holiday season's festivities, as they had "answered my call for a chair befitting the stature of Santa. Not only did they allow us to use their large, heavy wooden lodge chair, but they delivered it and picked it up. They definitely saved the day and provided the perfect seat for Santa."

Considering the way everything with the Glen House had played out (and his own somewhat magnanimous reasons for being zoning inspector), Zopf was dismayed that the leeway he granted property owners apparently went unappreciated. No concession is without criticism: people trying to building something get upset when Zopf says their plans aren't compliant with code; somebody complains that a B&B is violating code, and Zopf gets pilloried for not enforcing it. In those cases, Zopf said, it isn't his job to take a vote about what residents want—when it comes down to it, the answer is already outlined in code. Sometimes he just has to lay down the law.

The conflict between property owner and zoning inspector is sometimes a rivalry in the classic sense, like that of a dog and a mailman, or a hunter and a game warden. In disputes with the township, citizens are eager to cite the code back at officials with a smug look on their face, much like atheists when they quote a Bible verse at a fundamentalist in a way that implies immense satisfaction at using your opponent's own tools against them. But the counterarguer's victorious smirk is premature because nobody realistically knows more about code (or the Bible) than those who have based their lives around upholding it; no matter how fervent the protest or clever the perceived loophole, no outsider is going to be able to overrule an inspector's expertise. Erik Owen tried this tactic with Zopf, confidently citing various statutes throughout the duration of the conflict. Even though Owen's protestations

---

36. One couple who were part of the senior shoveling project said they "would like to shovel more than they do [but they worry] they might offend people who would read their action as an obligation or an admonishment for not shoveling themselves."

proved not to carry much weight, the fervor of his challenges led to what Zopf said was easily the most contentious zoning dispute of his career. Zopf said he has never had to truly "fight" with any-body—historically, he and the disputer always been able to talk and shake hands, he said—but the Glen House Inn situation was a different beast altogether. "Erik was unable to not push the lim-its," Zopf said, though he also agreed that the anti-inn neighbors weren't innocent either, as calling in a zoning inspector can be a vindictive strategy to get someone to stop doing something.

But even when a citizen of the township gets his way in a zon-ing issue, sometimes even that success isn't enough to temper the indignation at perceived governmental overreach. In January 1999, for example, a township resident named Harold Stancliff accused the zoning inspector and the trustees of inconsistency in their enforcement of township ordinances. The reason for his beef? A historic sign posted by the Village of Clifton across the street from Stancliff's home was too big. To be fair, the sign mea-sured sixteen feet square and was ten feet from the road, quali-ties that technically made it noncompliant. But even though W. W. "Bill" Deaton, the zoning inspector at the time, agreed with Stan-cliff and mandated that Clifton take down the sign, the victory wasn't enough. Stancliff lambasted officials at the meeting, making the perennial suggestion that some kind of collusion was afoot, or at least that there was "more than meets the eye" when it came to sign enforcement.

Stancliff cited numerous examples throughout the township that he said were out of compliance with zoning code: a trailer being used as an office space at a sewage treatment plant and a sign for a Boy Scout camp. What about these violations? It had taken three years to get a ruling on the Clifton sign—why weren't other signs being given the same scrutiny? Mucher said code enforce-ment had nothing to do with the content of the signs (though code makes no mention of the content of signs, just their mea-surements) but more to do with the logistics of physically inspect-ing every sign in the township. "We're not picayune enough to go out and check every sign," Mucher said after the meeting.[37] Zopf

---

37. The same meeting included discussion of a faulty Clifton tornado siren that went off in conjunction with the siren in Xenia. The sirens could be acti-vated by remote, and apparently the radio antenna was picking up both signals, or the one from Xenia but not Clifton.

agreed, saying that the township has never gone out and looked for violations to report. Typically, when someone brings a violation to light, he said, it is because it's causing a problem and the homeowner is too timid to talk with the offending neighbor in person. In Stancliff's case, it was the Village of Clifton that was causing a problem, and, based on the official ruling, the village took down its sign. After making his exasperation known at the meeting, it is not known how much longer Stancliff fumed about the inconsistent enforcement.

After Zopf delivered his brief business at the September 9 meeting and Hayden outlined her plans for the infamous letter, it was clearly getting to be time to draw the meeting to a close. There was nothing more anyone wanted to say about the B&B issue, and there were no modern-day Stancliffs present to draw attention to an oversized sign. They could sense the meeting was about to over, and they wanted to direct it to that end. After the meeting, Zopf would continue to be zoning inspector, a job he knew through and through, though at that point he had probably resolved to make sure he was more resolute in his decisions and perfectly clear about what was acceptable and what was not. The meeting had been a learning experience, a crash course, a dressing down, and a performance review, all rolled into one, and a pivotal moment in Zopf's career.

CHAPTER 10

The Meeting Is Over

Considering the breadth of the trustees' duties, it stands to reason that sometime, somewhere, someone is going to have a problem with the way some official process is carried out or how the trustees rule on an issue. Occasionally, the trustees will be on the receiving end of an irate phone call or the slightly more common irate email, but the trustees are not ordinarily besieged with complaints or the advice of nonpoliticians interested in telling them how to do their job.

"Like most governmental bodies, if things are going right, you don't hear too much from residents," Crockett said.

But at the township trustee meeting on September 9, 2015, however, the trustees heard from around a dozen residents, many of whom came prepared to argue their point with charts, tax information, and any other document they were able to unearth. Objectively, the B&B problem was one of quaint vituperations, but subjectively it was a serious affair.

However, everyone in the MTFR meeting room was done thinking about it, at least for the time being. There was a concerted effort to get through the rest of the evening so that everyone could go home and decompress. Following the citizen arguments, the presentation by Marty Heide, and the reading of the correspondence, the fire department report, the cemetery report, the fiscal officer's report, and then the zoning inspector's report, the night's final items—(9) the Standing Committee Report, (10) New Business, and (11) Old Business—were glossed over because there wasn't anything to mention. Following the conclusion of these items, the meeting was mercifully drawn to a close.

"Anything else before the board this evening?" asked Mucher. "No? Hearing that, I entertain a motion to adjourn."

"I make that motion," said Crockett.

"I second it," said Mucher.

"And by affirmation, we are adjourned," he said.

And that was it. The Miami Township Board of Trustees meeting of September 9, 2015, was over. It ran one hour, twenty-eight minutes, and forty-three seconds. It was approximately the 330th meeting the three trustees and the fiscal officer had conducted together. But if the trustees wanted to keep attending these meetings, they would have to work for it. Elections were coming up, and two trustee seats were up for grabs.

"No other Township . . . can claim as many acres of Township land protected from development"

As historian Michael Broadstone referred to them, the area's "useful citizens" continue to develop the township up through the present day. "The people of Miami Township respect the past while planning for the future," says the township's website, and one way they have planned for the future is by protecting land. "No other Township in Greene County or for that matter, in the Miami Valley, can claim as many acres of Township land protected from development," the website continues. Residents of Miami Township are perhaps more concerned about the township's environmental well-being than are the residents of the average township, having engaged in a number of green campaigns with characteristic integrity and aplomb.

Yellow Springs was spared the indignity of a garbage dump in its midst when its trash-collection practices were amended in the mid-1900s. The change was not only a smart choice in terms of the health of its residents but also a transformation that helped solidify the village's reputation as a forward-thinking green space. In 1951, the Yellow Springs League of Women Voters took issue with the state of local garbage collection, which at the time was collected by privately run horse-drawn carts and uncovered trucks, which carried their putrid loads up and down the streets of town and deposited them at a dumpsite that was basically in the middle of the village. The league consulted with experts and studied the practices of hundreds of other towns, eventually getting a resolution passed that mandated that garbage be collected by covered trucks and taken to a landfill far away from town.

Today, 3,500 acres of public and private land are under conservation easements, a legal standing that safeguards the land in perpetuity from development or being parceled out into smaller lots and sold. Farmland or forest, the easement stays with the property's deed. In 1998, citizens from Yellow Springs and other areas of the township and surrounding areas banded together to raise the millions of dollars needed to buy a historic, 950-acre property called Whitehall Farm and put it under a conservation easement. Trustee Chris Mucher helped organize the sale, which got pretty confusing as the acreage was divided into thirty-one lots that could be bid on separately, together, or in bits and pieces. Contributions to help buy the land came in many forms, including proceeds from bake sales to coffee-can donations to benefit concerts to a generous $3.275 million check written by a wealthy township couple. Once enough money was raised to buy the property, it was purchased and then sold at about half-price to a nonprofit that sets up land trusts, ensuring that the substantial acreage remain free from development forever. "Had the [couple] not stepped in, the area would likely be all houses," Mucher said.

Around the same time that the Save the Whitehall Farm campaign was going on, townspeople were rallying around another sacred bit of nature in the middle of Yellow Springs. In 2001, the local restaurant and bar Ye Old Trail Tavern made the controversial decision to remove an ancient, two-trunked Osage orange tree from its property, which is right in the middle of downtown on Xenia Avenue, a street deemed one of the country's nicest. The tavern was likewise a historical entity, first a bakery and then a tavern that got its start when Yellow Springs was first being developed.[38] The tavern and the rest of downtown were built up around the tree, which a local naturalist said "preceded the historical record of when Osage orange trees were brought to Ohio." But the tavern's owner wanted to expand the business, putting in a patio, more seating, and a handicap-accessible entrance. Accord-

---

38. The tavern is said to be haunted by the ghost of the original owner, who stipulated that no spirits would be served there, no pun intended. Many employees have seen loaves of bread and other supplies flying off shelves in response to the violation of his postmortem wishes.

ing to his insurance company and architects working on the project, the tree had to go due to the potential damage it would cause to the building or the patrons eating beneath it on the new patio.

"I didn't wake up one morning and say, 'I want to remodel. These trees must go,'" said the owner's daughter and manager of the tavern. "If one of these trees falls . . . it will ruin me."

The prospect of the tree's removal, even for the benefit of a local business, saddened and outraged many village residents. A committee called the Ye Old Trees Committee was formed to determine how they might be able to persuade the owners to keep the tree. Pro-tree advocates were puzzled that the village did not have a "tree ordinance" or something else on the books that prevented private property owners from simply hacking down everything on their property if they were so inclined. The village should know better, said one resident.

"I don't believe those trees are just private property," said another. "They are beloved members of our community."

The tavern's owner was wary that the issue would go the way of many issues in Yellow Springs, which is to say that it would be "talked to death" and then dropped. He had a business to run, and so he was steadfast in his decision to have the trees removed before the issue was bogged down in bureaucracy and public forums. As it became more and more certain that the tree would have to go, advocates ramped up their efforts to save it. Vandals left messages in chalk outside the restaurant saying "Save this tree" and telling people not to eat there. "Getting attacked like I do hurts my feelings," the manager said.

At one point, students from Antioch College camped out in the tree and refused to come down. A local man named Terry was arrested for slipping behind the police cordon and throwing blankets up to the campers, an offense for which he spent a night in jail.

Despite the appeals of the tree committee, the tree was finally chopped down. With questionable taste, the incident is sometimes referred to as "Yellow Springs' 9/11," as the twin trunks went down with far-reaching reverberations. The tavern expanded and guests can eat outside on the patio where the majestic, double-trunked Osage orange tree stood long before any developers did. Many villagers still refuse to eat there more than fifteen years later, and indeed the tavern is known primarily as a restaurant for tour-

FIGURE 22. A few concerned individuals camped in an old Osage orange tree on the property of the Ye Old Trail Tavern in downtown Yellow Springs. Photo courtesy of the *Yellow Springs News.*

ists. (Terry, a local farmer, collects food waste from local restaurants for compost but refuses to take compost from the tavern.) A few local woodworkers tried to get wood from the tree, to no avail, and pieces of the once-statuesque tree are said to have sat in the yard of the tavern's owner for years, covered in brush, perhaps unhonored but mourned and still remembered.

Despite the loss of the trees and the lingering disappointment that such majestic landmarks aren't accorded the respect they deserve, Miami Township does have three expansive natural areas that can be enjoyed with little fear of their disappearance: John Bryan State Park, Clifton Gorge, and a part of the Glen Helen Nature Preserve.

The first park is named after John Bryan, an area resident who owned a successful pharmaceutical business in the mid-1800s (and the same man who built the enormous barn mentioned in Historical Interlude 2). Bryan also fancied himself an author and self-published a book of fables. When he tried to get the book into the library of the young Antioch College, it was rejected because it didn't have any religious value. Bryan was a staunch agnostic and found the rejection galling, so in order to spite the college, he began buying land adjacent to it and vowed to put it out of business. While he didn't succeed in driving away the college, he willed his land to the state for use as a park, provided that no religious services could ever take place on its grounds. The long arm of the Lord ultimately prevailed, however, when courts ruled that religious beliefs couldn't be banned from public land, but at least his wish for a beautiful park still stands.

Clifton Gorge, near Clifton, boasts two miles of majestic, otherworldly gorges formed by the rushing waters of melting glaciers. Now named the Little Miami, the river sits far below the snaking river, which goes through a number of narrow channels "apparently formed by the enlarging and connecting of a series of potholes in the resistant Silurian dolomite bedrock." Enormous "stump blocks" stand with imposing timelessness on the valley floor, huge chunks of cliffs that broke loose and tumbled below.

Glen Helen is a 1,000-acre, limited-access natural area, with miles of hiking trails and the eponymous Yellow Springs. It was previously the land on which numerous hotels and resorts were built, but the bulk of the land was given to Antioch in 1925 by Hugh Taylor Birch in memory of his daughter, Helen. Because the rest of their family had died, Hugh and Helen were very close. They were budding naturalists who loved to explore the glen and everything living in it. He bought 700 acres of land around Antioch College and in 1925 donated it to the school in memory of Helen when she too died far too young at age forty-two. The only stipulation was that the area be named after her. Since then, Glen Helen has become a protected nature preserve, with minimal trails and development designed to encourage the growth of natural flora and fauna.

During the summer of 2015, the Village of Yellow Springs voted to annex the part of the glen that was in Miami Township, mostly in order to mitigate jurisdictional issues when police or EMTs were called there. Part of the glen was under the jurisdiction of the Yellow Springs Police Department, while the part of it in Miami Township was serviced by the Greene County Sheriff's Department. Chris Mucher opined that the Ohio legal system makes it "virtually impossible" to deny an annexation procedure, especially if there is a compelling reason to be annexed, such as making it easier for the local police. (Recent laws were passed that gave townships a slight fighting chance to prevent an annexation, which was better than ten years ago when townships "ended up getting annexed like crazy," he said.)

Mucher understood the logic behind the annexation, but it was still a little sad to see it go. Some states allow townships to incorporate themselves as "charter townships," which protects them from annexation, but, alas, Ohio does not have this option. Miami Township's total land once again decreased, a tradition since the early 1800s.

Township Trustee Elections

Broadstone's *History of Greene County* mentions some of the area's earliest politicians, those prominent citizens who endeavored to take their influence and ideas to a larger arena. Two men, both named James Miller, lived between Yellow Springs and Clifton not long after the towns were founded. "In order to distinguish between the two," Broadstone writes, "their friends dubbed one of them 'Congress' Miller and the other 'Stand-by' Miller. The first named had a perennial desire to Congress—a desire which, by the way, was never gratified; the other was a sober and steady sort of a citizen with no political aspirations, and hence was well named 'Stand-by' Miller."

Although as far as can be determined, none of the present township trustees share their names with anyone else in the township, the political ambitions that defined Congress Miller are aspirations that endure in Miami Township in the present day. Chris Mucher and Lamar Spracklen were up for reelection in November 2015 and were each being challenged by relative newcomers. Mark Crockett's seat was not up for grabs until 2017, as he was reelected to office in 2013.

Mucher's seat was being challenged by Zo Van Eaton-Meister, a robust, talkative woman and professional mom who had grown up in Yellow Springs and returned to the village in 2009; and Don Hollister, a lifelong township resident, who, among many other posts, has been a Yellow Springs Village Council member, a board member of Friends Care (an assisted care facility), and a Boy Scout advisor.

Spracklen's situation was a little different, as his seat was filled through special circumstances. Like Congress Miller, John Eastman had run for numerous offices without success until he won a township trustee position in 2013. However, Eastman tragically died from a heart attack one year into his term, and Spracklen was selected by the other trustees to replace him. Spracklen was finishing out the appointed term, and the election in November would appoint a permanent replacement to that chair.

Amstutz, a Miami Township farmer and Zoning Commission member, had chosen to run against Spracklen specifically. Rumor had it that there was some animus between Amstutz and Spracklen and that Amstutz's candidacy, while of course rooted in a serious commitment to the community, was also a bid to personally unseat Spracklen. Nobody could speak to the exact nature of their rivalry, but the difference between the size of their farms and the practices necessary to run them was suggested as one point of contention.

Soon enough, the public would get to scrutinize the candidates firsthand. The five trustee candidates—Mucher, Spracklen, Hollister, Amstutz, and Zo Van Eaton-Meister—were scheduled to debate in a candidate forum on October 22, 2015, set to take place in the gymnasium of the local elementary school.

Elections were on the customary first Tuesday in November, approximately two months away from the meeting on September 9. According to Ohio law, anybody can register to run for trustee. In order to do so, the prospective candidate first goes to the County Board of Elections in Xenia and gets a petition to run. After making sure the proper form is correctly filled out, the candidate has to collect at least twenty-five (but no more than seventy-five) valid signatures from the electorate. After signatures have been collected, the candidate returns the paperwork, pays a $30 fee, and is eligible to run. Candidate signs aren't supposed to be posted any sooner than thirty days before Election Day.

Chris Mucher, who had run in five elections before the 2015 cycle, had the process down pat. He reactivated chrismucher.com and updated it with recent stats and information. There was an ad to run in the *Yellow Springs News*, and he was wondering if new tactics were necessary to maintain his edge: "Four years ago, I bought 500 nail files with 'Mucher for Trustee' on them," he said. "I sent them out with letters so every time someone filed their nails they would think of voting for Mucher. My wife didn't think it was a good idea."

Long-serving trustees are recognized each year at the Ohio Township Association's annual convention. The number of people who remain in office after twenty, thirty, and even forty years is not unsubstantial. While Mucher said he didn't think he'd run indefinitely, he did say he would keep running as long as he felt he was still contributing to the township and was enthusiastic about the position, though becoming a trustee on the board of the Ohio Trustee Association is something he might consider further down the road as well.

Don Hollister printed fliers with his resume on one side and a fun township quiz on the other. He paid $200 to include an insert in almost 2,000 issues of the *Yellow Springs News*. Both items said "Paid for by Don Hollister" in small print at the bottom, as Ohio law requires the name of the person or entity who paid for the ad to be in a conspicuous place.

Van Eaton-Meister said anyone in town who knows you're running starts asking you about it right away. In the grocery store and on the street, people will come up to you and ask you about your positions or your campaign strategy. Somehow they immediately know when you file the paperwork, she said. The questioning is so frequent that she has a little fun with it. "I want to be serious because I want to win, but one of the first things I say when people ask me why I'm running is 'global domination.' You've got to start somewhere, right?"

But more seriously, her interest in the position comes from a place of care for her neighbors. "Nothing is more important to me than the health and safety of our community," read one of her campaign fliers. The land must be protected, she wrote, and she is an advocate of a "no sprawl" philosophy. She characterizes herself as "patriotic, but spiritual- and global-thinking." She is a trained therapist and imagines her intuition and understanding of the human organism would serve the trustee position well.

Van Eaton-Meister had embarked on an admittedly half-hearted run the year before. That was the year Eastman passed away and the coveted trustee position opened up. As a result, she said, anyone who had ever wanted to run did, including herself. Her cam-

Vote Nov 3rd

Don Hollister

for Miami Township Trustee

Don has been a lifelong Miami Township resident. His parents met as Antioch students. His grandparents retired here for 20 years. Don raised two daughters in Yellow Springs and is now a grandfather to 5 grandsprouts (alas, in Columbus).

Past local service:
Boy Scout Explorer Post Advisor
Plan Commissioner – Yellow Springs Village
Village Council – Yellow Springs
Glen Helen - Interim Director
YS Chamber of Commerce President
Tecumseh Land Trust Board member
Friends Care Center Board Member
Carpenter/independent contractor 13 years
Carpentry instructor, Greene Career Center

Currently:
Development Coordinator, Arthur Morgan Institute for Community Solutions
Greene Co. Community Fdn Board member

Paid for by Don Hollister,   Street, Yellow Springs, OH 45387

FIGURE 23A. Front of a Don Hollister election flyer from the 2015 elections. From the author's collection.

paign started out with vigor, but her enthusiasm waned after a fairly harrowing personal incident. Her 2015 bid was influenced partly by her frustrations with the how the event was handled.

One Sunday in October 2014, she was pushing her nineteen-month-old daughter in a carriage down the Little Miami bike path. It was 1:00 in the afternoon, and while she always slightly had her guard up, there was no reason to be unduly worried about

Know Your Township quiz

1. Which villages are included in our Miami Township of Greene County, Ohio?
a. Cedarville, b. Clifton, c. Jamestown, d. Yellow Springs

2. What rough percentage of Miami Township land area is in active agricultural use?
a. 50% b. 60% c. 70% d. 80%

3. Approximately how many miles of road does Miami Township maintain?
a. 8 miles b. 10 miles c. 12 miles d. 14 miles

4. How many incidents did the Township Fire Department and Rescue squad respond to during the year 2012?
a. 367 b. 783 c. 1088 d. 1137

5. How many active cemeteries does Miami Township maintain?
a. one b. two c. three d. four

6. In 2000 the population of the township was 5106. Did the population go up or down by 2010?
a. up b. down

7. What frontiersman is reported to have escaped Shawnees by leaping the Clifton Gorge?
a. Daniel Boone, b. Cornelius Darnell, c. Simon Kenton

8. The Yellow Spring is orange. Why is it called "yellow?"
☺ ☺

9. Whose name is on the other side of this sheet of paper?

answers: 1. b&d, 2. c, 3. c, 4. c, 5. b, 6. b, 7. b, 8. ☺

FIGURE 23B. Back of a Don Hollister election flyer from the 2015 elections. From the author's collection.

walking on a public path in the middle of the day. She was walking back toward Yellow Springs and was about a half-mile outside of town when she crossed paths with three young men, two of them on bikes and one on foot. They passed each other, and then the guys turned around and started following her. She walked a little faster; so did they. Then she took off running, pushing the carriage, and the men began chasing her. One of the guys started yelling, "Why are you running?" she said, taunting her.

"I don't really scare easily," she said. "I really thought my life was over."

They chased her down the bike bath. She had her phone with her and held it aloft as she was running.

"The only thing I said to these motherfuckers was, 'I'm married to a cop and I'm dialing 911!'"

They apparently thought she was videotaping them as she ran, she said, and this is what made them fall back. Fortunately, she was running toward town, and she started yelling the names of everyone who lived close by. She cut through a nearby fence and flagged down a police officer.

"Motherfuckin' assholes," she said. "Completely insane assholes from hell."

The incident shook her up pretty badly, and it happened three days before last year's televised candidate forum. She didn't know if she was up to doing the debate, but ultimately she chose to participate. It was good for her, she said, because it gave her something to focus on. Unfortunately, her mom suddenly got sick, and taking care of her took precedence. Her mother ended up being OK, but Van Eaton-Meister didn't have the time or energy to follow through with an effective campaign.

When the votes were tallied after elections a few weeks later, Van Eaton-Meister was happy to see she didn't come in last place. She said that if her mom didn't try to die on her again—"it's not like she hasn't done it before"—she would run again the following year. And there she was—a viable candidate in 2015.

The James A. McKee Foundation's Candidate Forum

The candidate forum was held in the gym of the Mills Lawn Elementary School in Yellow Springs on October 22. Not much was happening fifteen minutes before the debate was scheduled to begin. A few students sat in the back doing homework at a lunch table, and another group of students walked in wearing gym clothes, expecting to play basketball.

But people slowly trickled in, as did the techs responsible for setting up the PA system. Once the evening's attendees had arrived, it was clear that at least 90 percent of the audience was over sixty five years old. One audience member wore a pin that said "The death penalty is a hate crime." There were a lot of vacant seats, and more than a few of the attendees were incensed at the relatively small attendance. Two reporters from the *Yellow Springs News* sat in the audience, and they were quickly set upon by some of the attendees who asked why the *News* forgot to run an announcement about the candidate forum in the Community Calendar section of the paper. "I'd like to have a word with the editor of the paper," one woman said, hinting very transparently that this oversight was responsible for the scanty turnout.

Once everyone got settled, the moderator read the rules. Also debating that night were candidates for the Yellow Springs Village Council, as well as the mayor of Yellow Springs and a school board member, who were both running unopposed.

The trustee candidates would have five minutes to introduce themselves and respond to the three questions they'd been given in advance:

- How do you feel about building a new firehouse, and how will it be paid for?
- What do you think about requiring specific township trustee seats to be filled by residents who live in the township, outside of Yellow Springs? (Only Spracklen lived in the township proper; the other candidates all lived in Yellow Springs.)
- What can the township trustees do to help retain the rural character of the township?

"After five minutes," the moderator said, "the timekeeper will remove you with his hooked cane." The timekeeper, who actually did have a cane for personal use, smiled and held the implement aloft.

The audience could ask further questions of the candidates by writing them on a small note card that would be collected and read aloud by the moderator. He asked that the audience members please sign the questions so they would know they were coming from a real person and noted that questions could be edited on the fly to reduce personal attacks.

David Foubert, the mayor of Yellow Springs, spoke first. The moderator welcomed Foubert, though he noted that the mayor wasn't feeling well. The audience laughed, as the mayor was onstage in front of him. "Well, he's doing well for a politician," the moderator said.

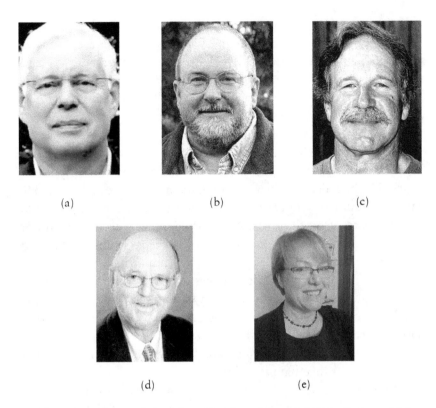

FIGURE 24. Politicians of Miami Township, past and present: (a) John Eastman, (b) Don Hollister, (c) Dale Amstutz, (d) Yellow Springs mayor Dave Foubert, and (e) Zo Van Eaton-Meister. Photos courtesy of the *Yellow Springs News* and the author's collection.

Foubert was running uncontested. He had been mayor for twenty-four years and was recognized mainly as the Ceremonial Head of Village and Proclamations. One of his duties as mayor is to deliver proclamations, he said, though he did oversee the town's mayor's court, a juryless court in which the mayor had the power to hear misdemeanor cases and dispense punishments. During his speech, Foubert expounded upon why sending low-level offenders to mayor's court rather than the county municipal court in Xenia benefited the town: it arguably made for a more community-oriented approach to policing versus sending someone into the impersonal maw of a larger court system. He spoke for awhile and squinted at the time clock. "What does that say? Thirty seconds? Ten? OK." He counted down from ten. "Three . . . two . . . one. Aaaand goodnight!" he said. He left the stage after thanking the moderator for allowing him to speak at his mother's funeral.

The township trustee candidates sat onstage all the while. Mucher sat relaxed, his legs slightly splayed, turning a coffee cup around in his hand. He was wearing his customary khakis and white button-down shirt. Spracklen sat with his standard glare, ready to get it over with. The challengers, Amstutz, Hollister, and Van Eaton-Meister, fidgeted just a little, not quite used to the public-speaking duties the office entails.

Amstutz went first. He introduced himself as having worked at a grain elevator and the post office for the past twenty-seven years. He had degrees in farm management and economics. He said he would buy land for a new firehouse and would sell old properties to offset the costs. As a farmer, he was concerned about the rural community not getting adequate representation. He had "nothing negative to say about anyone running," but noted that Xenia Township requires its trustees to live within its boundaries. Amstutz had been on the Zoning Commission for fifteen years and knew code front to back, knowledge that would help him preserve the rural character of the township.

"I live in the country for a reason," he concluded. "I love growing crops and I love having animals."

Hollister was next. He thanked the foundation for hosting the event, the audience for being there, and all the candidates for running for office. He addressed the "elephant in the room," the question of building another firehouse. "I don't know," he said. "The township has been a little too cautious in building it. We have the cash, why not buy a plot? I don't know. It's a bit of a local mystery." He noted that the township needed more videos of its meetings on the web, to foster better communication with the constituents. As to preserving the rural character, he would welcome agricultural prospects, including niche markets that would help farmers continue to make money. He agreed with Amstutz that a farmer on the board would serve the township's interests better.

Hollister's answers were a little stilted, and he occasionally seemed slightly befuddled. He had a habit of saying "I don't know" between thoughts. He was, however, one of only two candidates who answered the questions they were supposed to answer. Following Amstutz and Hollister presentations, the evening's dialogue quickly veered off on three separate, fairly unrelated courses according to who was speaking.

Chris Mucher was next, the candidate with the most experience. He stepped forward into a well-placed single spotlight that seemed to follow him around as if he was in a one-act play. His hands were folded in front of him, and he took a short breath before speaking.

"I'm not about sitting back and putting my feet up . . . ," he began. The audience *Oooohed* because Spracklen was sitting with his feet up. Then Mucher looked serious and said he was going to go off-topic and get more personal.

"There's more to being trustee than people think. It's about crunching numbers, getting up in the middle of the night to plow or saw a dead tree," he said. "This town has literally put food on my table, and I want to repay the township."

His eyes scanned the room, beseeching, his hands opening in appeal to the crowd. The speech he gave highlighted his experience and his seriousness and appealed to the audience's sense of practicality. It did not directly answer any of the questions, but he did make a compelling case for his reelection.

Spracklen was next, sauntering up to the mic and gripping the sides of the podium.

"I've been a farmer all my life, like both sides of my family before me," he began. "The word 'choice' comes to mind. We make choices every day but don't often give thought to it."

He too chose not to address any of the questions directly, though he gave an eloquent speech that often returned to the theme of 'choice.' He had notes but didn't consult them. The township's rural character would be respected because the township appoints members of the BZA, he said. He then sat back down.

Despite his gruff demeanor—*Yellow Springs News*'s coverage of the elections consistently mention Spracklen not returning requests for comment—Crockett said Spracklen is a trustee because he has knowledge and expertise that will help the community. As a lifelong farmer, Spracklen had knowledge of agriculture that was totally unmatched by any of the other officials. When drainage becomes an issue in some of the fields in the township, Spracklen gets to work. "That's just what he does," Crockett said later. "He's not in it for the money."

The butterflies in Zo Van Eaton-Meister's stomach were fluttering as she approached the mic. She chuckled nervously and began. "A lot of people don't know this, but I'm very patriotic," she said.

She referred to notes she had prepared, but the stress of speaking in front of a crowd redirected her remarks. Her speech was effectively a biography, highlighting her experience in grad school and her unexpected career as a therapist. "I quickly found my niche in the legal system as a county-designated mental health professional. We don't have them here in Ohio but they have them in Alaska," she said. There was a sense of wonder in the air regarding when her speech would loop back around to something pertaining to trusteeship. She was going through the ups and downs of her years away from the area when the timekeeper called "time." She tried to continue and he called "stop" again.

The timekeeper had been irate the whole evening, and his temper flared when people went over their allotted time by even a few seconds. Van Eaton-Meister was playing fast and loose with the timer, and he wasn't having it. "THANK YOU *VERY MUCH*," he said.

"My god, five minutes goes fast," she said, finally seeing the sign he was waving. "People fear public speaking more than death. It's a good thing when you don't die."

She sat back down. With the township candidates' prepared speeches taken care of, the emcee said he would take further questions from the audience. The note cards with written questions were slow in coming, but finally some made their way to the front.

The first question asked for clarifications about which candidates were running for two-year terms. Next was a question about influence of a project like the Center for Business and Education (CBE) on the rural character of the township. (The CBE was a contentious and somewhat ill-fated development project that got voted out of existence in 2013.) Hollister pointed out that CBE land was annexed into Yellow Springs and thus wasn't a threat to the township's character. It was a "rural project incubator," but, in the manner of his earlier five-minute speech, he said he didn't know about available money to invest or how to invest it. Amstutz agreed that most development was primarily in urban areas; Mucher said only, "Dale read my mind," and passed the mic, an abrupt response that elicited an awkward laugh from the audience. Spracklen said he was successful in getting farmers on the Zoning Commission, and Van Eaton-Meister said while development shouldn't be nonexistent, it should be well-thought-out. She also added that she's been to Hawaii, Alaska, and the San

Juan Islands and thought that Miami Township was just as beautiful as any of these places.

The final question of the evening concerned township land being annexed by the Glen Helen Nature Preserve. Was the loss of some acreage a good thing for the township? Mucher considered it a "net neutral" transaction—the township doesn't have to maintain land that wasn't bringing revenue. "I'm not into losing land," he said, but he felt overall that it was a good thing because the glen will get the policing that it needs from the village of Yellow Springs. (Recall that Glen Helen was previously served by different police departments because it straddled Yellow Springs and township boundaries.) Spracklen simply said he didn't have a problem with it, prompting someone in the audience to say, admiringly, "There's a man of few words." Hollister agreed it was a good thing, as did Van Eaton-Meister, who said there were no drawbacks, and the promise of a quick police response was a benefit for visitors to the glen.

With those three questions, the township trustee segment of the community forum drew to a close. They stayed sitting onstage as the uncontested school board member gave his speech, all smiling, transmitting to the audience that intentions of the board were pure and that their relationship to the township was one of genuine regard. November 3 was only a few weeks away.

In the weeks leading up to the election, Van Eaton-Meister would be seen in front of one of Yellow Springs' coffee shops, sitting at a table with campaign literature; Hollister's fliers would be inserted into an upcoming newspaper, and Spracklen wouldn't do much in the way of campaigning. His experience spoke for itself. Mucher placed an ad in the paper, and Amstutz put up a few signs. They did what they could and hoped voters would recognize their sincerity and the unique skills they would bring to the table.

Lamar Spracklen and Chris Mucher were soundly reelected. Mucher took 44 percent of the votes in his race, though Don Hollister trailed by only 143 votes. Spracklen took 65 percent of the votes in his race and began a new four-year term. Amstutz still sits on the Miami Township Zoning Commission.

The Miami Township Board of Trustees continues to hold meetings the first and third Mondays of every month, generally at 7 p.m. The public is always invited to attend.

FIGURE 25. The front page of the *Yellow Springs News* announcing the winners of the 2015 elections. Courtesy of the *Yellow Springs News*.

Unintended Consequences

An Essay about Community[39]

By Deann Ward

Yellow Springs, Ohio

Neighborhoods are collections of diverse individuals living in close proximity, all with their own ideas about what constitutes neighborly behavior. Each neighbor exhibits behavior they find acceptable and justified on any given day while those next door may see it differently.

One cannot know that the community you have joined is a peacefully functioning place until some time passes, some life happens. A sense of true community in a neighborhood is a product of the interactions people experience collectively. When folks in a neighborhood have a live and let live attitude, community is much easier to cultivate.

When people expect the best of one another, that is mostly what they get. When I came here, I brought an expectation that all of my neighbors could behave in such a way that everyone else could live as they chose, and ultimately, act toward one another from what Marilynne Robinson calls "—an imaginative love for those we do not really know." Actions from such underlying love create and sustain community.

Out on the Circle

A villager might ask, "where do you live?" to which I would reply, "out on Grinnell Circle." "Oh, that is such a nice area!" And I would say, "yes,

---

39. This essay has been reprinted exactly as it originally appeared with any errors retained.

thank you, I feel quite fortunate to live there." Recently, the questioner responds quite differently. "Oh! What is going on out there? Why can't you people get along?" Seems everyone on the Circle has been painted with the same brush by the conflicts about the Glen House Inn.

In late September, 2015, as a result of action taken by some, but not all, of the residents living contiguous to the Glen House Inn, a group of seven governmental representatives, including a county prosecutor, served a cease and desist letter to Erik and Deirdre Owen at their YS home, the Glen House. A neighborhood where folks had tended to be tolerant and friendly was transformed that day into US vs. THEM. A YS News report on October 1 stated that the action was a victory for some of the inn's neighbors who have been expressing concern for years that the activity of the inn has been disruptive to the neighborhood. For some perhaps. Not for all. To me, it is a very painful outcome given all the good that's been lost.

When I moved here in 1998, I found the Circle neighborhood functioned by fits and starts in a peaceful manner. I also purchased a financial connection to all my neighbors in the form of the shared water system. I didn't give that aspect of buying my house much thought until I eventually realized all the neighbors were deeply tied to my property. Interacting and getting along was going to be required.

Mostly, neighbors wanted to be left alone. Bill Hooper managed the water system as a benign dictator, most were grateful for his role as the last of the founding members of this subdivision. Back then, a derelict vehicle on the Millers' lot might have been an exasperating eyesore to the neighbors, but nothing was said as long as live and let live was tacitly observed. Or a long term remodeling project may have been a creative process or a matter of getting more money together while representing a perceived damper on property values and an unwanted eyesore for others. Still, live and let live prevailed. Items stored strategically on one owner's property due to lack of storage buildings was an ongoing irritant one learned to overlook while driving by because we were forgiving of one another. People lived with the normal irritations caused by living among neighbors, hoping to get the same measure of tolerance each gave. I called it a Yellow Springs way of being.

That has changed.

I am writing about this change because I am in the position of interacting regularly with all my neighbors as one of the volunteer managers of our water system. I am writing because I hope to provide overlooked information publicly and, I hope, a way for everyone to step back, re-evaluate and choose again, perhaps choose for peace and tolerance.

Let's examine the complaints brought against the Owen home, the Glen House Inn, in the hope of creating a way to understand one another. The primary complaints were increased traffic, increased exposure of the neighborhood and extra noise connected to a limited number of paid special events held at the inn.

Increased Traffic

One issue raised is the number of cars driving the complete circuit of Grinnell Drive before entering the driveway for the inn. "Why would they do that?" asked a neighbor. Well, it is a public roadway. It is how a buyer will find your home when you try to sell. It is how I found my home when I naively turned onto this unfamiliar road one January day. I was following my intuition and because I did, within three months, I was living here next to the South Glen! Motorists may be following their intuition. Glen Road and Grinnell Drive are not private access roads, these are Miami Township roadways.

Seeing others on the Circle has always been enjoy able for me. Sometimes I'd see Bob Parker making the circuit or the Hatfield sisters or a bus from Friends' Care out to provide a scenic ride for residents. Sometimes, it has been Mr. Chappelle. And I have to admit that gives me a thrill so, thanks, Dave; that is me bashfully waving from my garden. I wave at everyone to be neighborly, out of a sense that sharing this place is a form of gratitude for the privilege of living here. Any lovely weekend, there are tourists finding the Circle for the first time who wave and smile back when greeted. There are folks looking for the inn or that covered bridge in the Glen or are simply curious about this lovely place. I do not see vehicles circling in our neighborhood as an immediate safety concern; I see potential friends behind the wheel.

Bed and breakfast guests often used navigational technology to find the Glen House Inn. Initially, those tools did not send guests directly to the inn but to its general vicinity. Guests drove into the Circle without adequate help to find the inn's driveway. The roadway pitches the driver to the right upon entering the Circle which means guests missed the sign for the inn, a sign which was inconspicuous because that was the demand of zoning regulations and some neighbors from the outset. Having made the entire circuit without finding the inn, guests often turned down Glen Road in hopes of finding the inn and, instead, encountered a dead end and no Glen House. I have been fortunate to have many cordial conversations with such folks. What I found fortunate was unwelcome for others. I am sorry that the traffic and the strangers were a source of fear and discomfort for some of my neighbors. Truly sorry. I imagine they have legitimate reasons for feeling unwelcoming. For this reason, a new road sign went up restricting access to Glen Road plus, over time, the GPS companies improved their apps with repeated prompts by the Owens for more precision.

Increased Exposure and Noise

The Owen family joined the neighborhood about 2005. The story goes that Erik and Deirdre were traveling in Europe as young, idealistic artists when they sketched a dream home on a cocktail napkin at a sidewalk café. Years later, they would build that home on a lot next to, but not a part of, the Grinnell Subdivision, therefore, their property was not subject to the same deed restrictions as our properties. First, the Owens restored the Grinnell historic barn on the property as their temporary home.

That is the same barn that provided a temporary home to people who waited for their cabins to be completed closer to Yellow Springs, people who had escaped slavery in Virginia in 1862. While living in that barn, those newly free were closer to realizing their dreams, something the Owens were also experiencing. That old barn had been neglected for years, the property was deteriorating, de pressing property values for everyone nearby. The restoration of the barn gave the historic site a new lease on life. What a happy result! Then, the Owen dream house went up, largely by their own hands.

I am not so different from the Owen family. When I moved to the Circle, even though I am an introvert, my first impulse was to share my home. I housed people overnight, hosted gatherings, sponsored retreats, and increased the traffic, the noise and the exposure of the neighborhood. I didn't ask anyone's permission. I didn't check deed restrictions. Only one set of neighbors complained to me, threatening to call the sheriff. Therefore, I strongly resonated with the Owen family filling their dream home with parties, art, music, good food and joy long before they conceived of the Glen House Inn.

I loved sharing this place and was rewarded with the people I met and events held here. Imagine having had all these joyful events in one home: the Bahá'í community's monthly devotional gatherings; Antioch University faculty meetings; baby showers; farewell dinners for conflict-resolution cohorts; workshops; house concerts; crone ceremonies;

solstice vigils; and dinner for Antioch students with Nobel Peace Prize laureate José Ramos Horta. It was all magical. It likely contributed to increased traffic, noise and exposure while creating extraordinary experiences for my guests and me. That is an essential point: when people gathered in this space, magic happened that transformed everyone involved. The Owen home provided just such a space, too.

I distinctly remember the afternoon I was out walking when I ran into Erik who invited me over for an "arts night." Even if I wasn't artistic, it was going to be a night to remember and I was welcome. The Owen family brought that kind of joy to their home and the neighborhood. Like me, they may have contributed to the irritants of increased traffic, noise and people on the Circle, sure, but the congeniality and shared experiences mitigated any inconveniences in my view.

When the Glen House Inn was announced in the YS News, it caught many neighbors by surprise. For some it was a pleasant surprise, for others it was alarming because it meant their quiet, private neighborhood was more exposed. Now, the Owens invited all neighbors to public gatherings at their home. An Art Open House was only a short walk away. Some of my neighbors would be out on the Circle walking over to the Owen home at the same time so we had a chance to chat, catch up on our personal lives. As a long time friend of the Owen family, my neighbor, Richard Simons asked me to write a letter to the editor last October in support of the inn for many reasons including Richard's report that the CMYS gatherings held at the inn were remarkable and greatly appreciated by that organization. Many groups and extended families in the community have benefitted from the inn and the generosity of the Owen family.

Politicians, artists, music, all were available at public events held at the inn. Many familiar, YS faces were present when I attended events. I am grateful that the Owen family made these events possible and available. It was neighborly. As Dan Rudolf was reported to have said in the previously referenced YS News article, he would rather have the inconvenience of a party once in a while than eliminate the benefit the inn brings to the community. I agree! However, at the same time, I am completely aware that for those neighbors whose homes are not air conditioned and had all windows wide open, for those whose homes lie along the creases in topography here which funneled sound directly into their open windows from the Glen House Inn, the celebrations were disconcerting, even maddening.

Enough

Attitudes hardened as the inn operations continued. Different inn keepers, different definitions of primary residence, different understandings of how the inn was expected to function followed. Fear, intolerance and anger appeared when nerves were frayed by a particularly loud, long, late night event. That one left the Owen family similarly frustrated by the lack of consideration for the inn's policies that one wedding party exhibited. That happened once.

Still, did my neighbors who objected to all events realize that events taking place at the Owen home were a mixture of what the family hosted on a regular basis that was not business in addition to hosting inn guests and limited events? I had done the same at my home. My neighbors entertain, have celebrations, garage sales, events that increase traffic and noise. Couldn't we extend to the Owen family the same tolerance that we expect when we hold an event at our own homes?

Long-simmering conflict became especially pronounced when rumors about the Owen property surfaced in 2015: there might be a party barn like Gilberts' on Trebein, viticulture, wine production, a tasting room and a liquor license. Tenants moved out of the barn, trees were felled beside the barn. Activities around the inn led to inaccurate assumptions. Having felt ignored, unheard during attempts to negotiate or complain in the past, unhappy neighbors mobilized to proactively block any of those rumored possibilities at the inn while fearing what might happen. According to the Owen family, none of those neighbors that initiated the actions by govern mental officials called them directly with questions about these rumors.

I was not a partner to the discussions with the Owens or their representatives to solve conflicts with concerned neighbors over the years. I was aware of the conflicts due to my role with the water system and ongoing conversations with all my neighbors. I made independent suggestions to resolve the issues such as engaging the Village Mediation program to work out conflicts, available at no cost to township residents, or using the giant ceramic pot at the entrance to the inn property as a destination marker for guests. Neither was I in the group that took formal action against the operations at the Glen House Inn, that informally called themselves the Concerned Circle Citizens, a name that sounds like everyone on the Circle was involved. Half the neighbors were. I tried but do not entirely understand why these neighbors felt they had to gather, plan, investigate the Owens and insist upon action through governmental agencies to stop developments at the inn on the Owen private property.

Unintended

What has happened as a result of these conflicts is that our neighborhood is now working with the US vs. THEM dynamic. Peace, inclusivity and cooperation have been damaged. Live and let live has been severely tested.

How could this situation have been handled differently for the Owens? by the Owens? for the neighbors? by the neighbors for whom uses of the Owen home, the Glen House Inn, became disruptions they couldn't tolerate?

Was thought given to the neighbors who enjoyed, profited from or had no quarrel with the inn's operation, who are friends of the Owen family, how they might react, how these actions taken to restrict family and inn operations would negatively impact the functioning of the neighborhood as a whole?

Now, the inn is for sale, the number of guests is severely and selectively limited, incoming revenue is not sufficient to sustain the property, the place where family and community gatherings could be held is no longer available, the historic barn is empty again. The infrequent jolts of celebratory energy that resulted from Owen family or Glen House Inn activity have mostly ceased. The traffic is lighter. Noise seems to be back to construction, gardening, lawn mowers and such. Some neighbors are no longer speaking, going out of their way not to encounter one another. Neighbors who hoped to have a wedding on the big field have given up the idea fearing a negative reaction from CCC members. Situations that used to be overlooked on other's property or in other's behavior are no longer off limits or forgiven. Building inspectors and the health department have been called to enforce compliance by neighbors whose choices would have been overlooked in the past. Some continue to harass the Owen family and the inn, seemingly trying to entrap them in misdeeds. Sheriff's deputies drive around the Circle more frequently. We can conclude the inn has been run imperfectly as most all human endeavors are: it benefited many; harmed some. Unfortunately, the Owen home and the inn has become a lightning rod for fear of one another.

These are only some of the many unintended consequences. Fear came to live on the circle. Fear and suspicion of others seems to tinge interactions now rather than imaginative love for those we do not know. The living organism that is this neighborhood is, for me, injured. I grieve deeply the loss of live and let live. How shall we collectively fix this situation and forgive? Now that people on the Circle have been called out for problematic behavior, how do we call one another back in to make this a place of peaceful co-existence once again? Only half the job is complete when we call others on behavior that injures. There is more to be done. How do we forgive, cast out all the past disagreements rather than holding that list so tightly and move on? How do we reinstate the Yellow Springs way of living together? I hope we may all learn to be better neighbors for one another by considering this situation on the Circle with imaginative love for those we do not really know.

Questions Remain

How does a neighborhood move forward after such divisiveness?

Why didn't we all talk to, listen to one another with an attitude of imaginative love for one another? with a sense of live and let live?

Why did we suspect the worst of one another and let fear color the way we see one another? What are we afraid of?

I spend time walking in the South Glen trying to figure out what I should do or not do to mend this Circle because I love it here, love the people here. First, maybe we as a community could utilize the Village Mediation Program and clear the air. Then maybe we could have a pot luck dinner or two and turn the anger and suspicion back toward familiarity. I don't consent to the unwelcome fear trying to sink its ugly roots in my beloved neighbor hood. There must be ways we can cultivate the sense of imaginative love for the unknown other here and disarm the antagonism.

Fear will not dictate how I will behave. I have learned that live and let live is a precious commodity, once dam aged, sorely missed and hard to reclaim. I really miss Bill Hooper.

Interviews with Miami Township Fire and Rescue Fire Chief Colin Altman and Lieutenant Nate Ayers

The following interviews were conducted in spring 2016 at the Miami Township Fire and Rescue firehouse. Chief Altman and Lieutenant Ayers were interviewed back-to-back in the chief's office.

Chief Altman:

I grew up in a town in New Jersey that had a very strong fire department and first-aid squad. My parents had friends on the squad. I always thought about joining the department as a volunteer, but I never did it. But then I came to college at Antioch, which had a student-run fire department. I fell in with the department toward the end of my first year on campus, partly because I never really fit in anywhere else on campus. It was a campus of weird people, and we were all weird in our own way.

At the time, MTFR required you to be both a firefighter and emergency responder. Firefighting didn't really interest me. So I begrudgingly took the firefighting class with the theory that I'd just drive the fire truck. Three days after we graduated from class and got our certifications, we got called to a fire in Cedarville. I had to go into the building with one of my partners, and the ceiling collapsed on me. I was trapped for a little bit, I hurt my shoulder and had to go to the hospital, and after that I fell in love with it. That experience made firefighting what I wanted to do.

I was at Antioch to be a psychologist, and I'm really happy that I'm doing this instead. I think I'd probably be strangling people if I had to be a psychologist. College was a struggle for me because I wasn't the most disciplined student anyway. I was one of those kids who probably would've benefited from a year off. I took a few years off for some extended co-ops [part of the Antioch experience is a cooperative learning program, typically in another state or country] and flirted with some other careers but really wanted to go back to firefighting. By the time I was done with college, I was twenty-five or so and had been a firefighter since I was seventeen. I'd gained progressively more experience, and then the job at MTFR opened.

My predecessor as fire chief was a wonderful guy, but he'd never been a volunteer firefighter, and he'd never worked with volunteers. There were some tumultuous times when he was here because he'd been a career firefighter his whole life. He was a union firefighter, which is a whole different world. Guys come into work because they are getting a paycheck versus guys coming in because they really want to be there—it's a different mindset. They thought I had the proper mindset to heal some of these wounds and take the department in a different direction. I still have a job, so it seems like I'm doing something right.

It comes down to how you manage and lead. In a place where everyone is getting paid to be there, it feels like a job. I'm not saying that guys who are full-time union firefighters don't love what they do, 'cause they do. But you have to keep in mind that most of the people here are volunteers. They're here for a variety of reasons, but it's not the paycheck. They're here to be firefighters. They saw a way to help their community, to give back, or even just a way to get out of the house—we have to have a philosophy that balances all of that and honors that commitment with the needs of our guys who are paid.

We provide all the training. The township pays for the firefighter training classes in May. It's about $1,000 per student to certify them. We provide the equipment. Candidates just have to give us time in return. We ask that they do at least thirty-two hours per month on the schedule once they've completed the training. But they schedule themselves. They log onto a website and sign up for the shifts they want. It's pretty simple. And they have to show up on Tuesday nights, 'cause that's our training night. They have to show up to 75 percent of those.

We have policies and procedures, obviously, and we expect people to follow them. But we don't really have a lot of problems. It's a good atmosphere—if someone screws something up, it's because they didn't know procedure. We rarely have to take corrective action, which is nice, because that's not my thing. I mean, if it has to happen, it has to happen, but if you can pull someone aside and explain to them that that's not the right way to do it, then that's much better than yelling at someone.

One of the things I love about this job is seeing the change in people. EMT classes are much more "book classes"; fire class is far more "[grunts and flexes]." Everyone thinks they can only push themselves so far, but one of the things we do in fire class is tear down that wall, push people beyond it. Because there are going to be times on the job when you're going to have to be physical. A baby is trapped or your partner is trapped, and you have to go beyond your limits. I love to see the change in people when they realize that they can do a lot more. For me, as an instructor, it's a great thing to see people grow physically, emotionally, and spiritually. I've seen everyone here really go through really positive and professional changes.

We have a very strong, very close relationship with the Yellow Springs Police. The YSPD comes on almost every call we do. They back us up. There is a traditionally a rivalry between cops and firefighters. We don't really have it here because we work so closely together, but we make jokes at each other's expense—the cops all want to be firemen, that kind of stuff. We work well with the Greene County Sheriff's Department and state patrol and state parks officers. We answer calls in other places, [as] there's a regional mutual aid contract. Greene County is actually very good about that. For instance, if we have a fire in Yellow Springs, an engine from Xenia Township is automatically going to be sent. We just went to Xenia Township a week and a half ago; they had a car crash and needed another truck. The computer pulls us up, we don't ask questions, we do what the dispatch center says and head out. It's a nice setup. We work really well together as fire departments in Greene County, and that's not always the case in a lot of places.

It's intense in a small community because you're going to know a lot. You know everybody, or at least recognize them, when you go on a call. We see a lot of scandalous stuff that you don't talk about. It's funny to read the perspectives in the paper or see what's on that insane Facebook group,[40] because sometimes it's like, this person isn't the saint you think they are. We want to, but of course we can't say that last week he was beating his wife.

---

40. Yellow Springs Open Discussion is a notorious Facebook group where area residents no have qualms in saying what's on their mind.

You definitely do build a wall around things so you don't have to deal with them. We see a lot of really cool things, and every now and then we get to save peoples' lives, but we also see a lot of suffering. You see the seedy underbelly of the area. It's the same as the police. We see domestic abuse, we see child abuse, we see drug use, and certain things are difficult to deal with. There are things that stick with you, that define your career, that are still difficult to talk about. We really encourage people to open up and talk about things like that, which is hard because we tend to attract people who are really stoic. But the more experienced members can talk to the younger ones, and hopefully help them through things. You certainly get haunted by a lot of things. I think at my level, or the assistant chief's level, or the captain's level, because you're in charge of things, you feel guilt, like why did this happen? How did this happen?

Typically it's on the ambulance side of things that we see most of the tragedy. I mean, the last [ones] that died in a fire here were chickens. People have their different triggers. I always think back to this one call. There was a young MTFR firefighter; he had experience with other departments but was brand new here, and he was on a routine transport for a cancer patient. She was very ill, it was very sad situation, and it devastated this kid. I didn't realize it at the time, but his grandfather was going through the same thing. There's always those connections that can hit you. I'm the same way. I wouldn't think a call would bother me but it did. It happens.

We have to watch because sometimes our staff can be too sympathetic, too empathetic. They'll want to hold hands and that kind of stuff [with someone who is hurt or scared], but that's not our job. It is a certain part of our job, but our job is getting you fixed, getting you to the hospital in one piece, and we can't distract ourselves with the human tragedy side of it. It's important to our patients that we're comforting—we hug a lot of people, we cry with people, but when the shit hits the fan, you've got to focus on doing your job and getting a person to the hospital. It definitely takes its toll. Especially with new people—you take them aside, ask them if they're OK, ask them if they understand what happened on a call. But there are people who are surprisingly OK. They'll experience their first death and be fine. You'll ask them if they're OK, and they'll say, Yeah, why? It's an interesting array of responses.

We have an interesting blend of people. We have people who have been volunteering for 15 years. We have Antioch students who are here for four years or so. We have a kid from Wittenberg [College] who comes down. He's got a finite period of time [because of school]. We also take people from outside the township who aren't served by a volunteer fire department.

But I don't think [the length with which people work as volunteers] is as long as it used to be. The single biggest change in my career as a fire fighter is the drop in the number of volunteers. That's the strongest factor affecting what we do. Smaller numbers means it's less safe for fire-fighters on a scene. When I started, when we responded to a fire alarm on the Antioch campus, all three fire engines would respond, each one full. Now we're lucky if we have one fire truck out. Sometimes a fire alarm is just a fire alarm, but sometimes it's a fire and [fewer people] makes the situation less safe.

We try to stay involved and at the forefront of safety and training. For years, firefighters had kind of a cowboy, yee-hah approach to the profession, but I think the other biggest change I've seen since I started is that now firefighting is really focused on safety. Both myself and the assistant chief are involved regionally and statewide in different fire-related things. We both chair different committees and sit on committees, and we really try to stay at the forefront and bring things back to the station, and keep our guys on top of stuff. There are national standards from the National Fire Protection Association that cover pretty much everything we do. They cover everything from the manufacture of our gear to operations on scene. The state has its own regulations from the Bureau of Workers' Compensation. On the medical side, we have standing orders that are developed by physicians. We follow those, take tests on those; they tell us how to treat patients.

We don't fight fire every day and we don't do a cardiac arrest every day, but we owe it to our community and our staff to make sure they're trained very well, that they're safe, that they have the best equipment they can. Sometimes that can be tough, because the best is sometimes expensive. You have to convince the public and elected officials that it's worthwhile. "Why do you want a new fire engine instead of something that's used?" Because our guys deserve the best. New stuff is not crazy-priced anyway, it's safe and is a stainless steel roll cage basically, and that's better than a 1982 hand-me-down.

We're much more aware now of the rates of cancer in firefighters. They're now predicting it's the number one killer of firefighters and not heart attacks, like we used to think. Burning plastic, diesel exhaust from the engines . . . I was at a seminar last week about cancer prevention and the numbers were just shocking. Male firefighters are more than three times more likely to develop testicular cancer than the average person.

They had pretty much had every cancer listed there, and firefighters were above the national average. It's an awakening that it's dangerous what we do. But it's not what people think. They think we run into burning buildings and they collapse on us. Which does happen, but most of the time we're dying because we're fat and out of shape, or because we have cancer or something horrible like that. That awareness has changed. And it's finally coming to light that there's a really high suicide rate among firefighters. Not here, luckily, but it's something that you always think about.

People's reactions to firefighters vary. Yellow Springs is such a strange little community. People will see us in uniform and are instantly turned off by that. They'll see us walking together and think we're some [authority] or something. But overall, people respect what we do even if they don't know who we are. Kids will wave at the fire trucks. When people realize we're here, they like us and respect us for what we do. People always say, "Wow, you got here so fast. Did you come from Xenia?" No, we're right in your own town. You vote for our levy!

Lieutenant Nate Ayers:

I'm a full-time lieutenant. I'm in charge of special operations here in Miami Township. I oversee rope-rescue and our pike team, stuff like that. Rope-rescue is climbing, rappelling, pulling people out of Clifton Gorge, doing pick-offs on cliffs. We have part of a truck dedicated to that. One of my first calls as a lieutenant, one of my first major calls, was three girls stuck in Clifton Gorge. They wanted to go cliff-diving and got themselves stuck down by the water. There was no way to get back up. It was so slick because it had been raining for days. I was like, "All right, this is fun."

I'm from Dayton and moved here when I was eighteen and started working with my father at Friends Care. I did maintenance there for three years. I'd never really thought about being a volunteer firefighter. Apparently our captain and my dad were talking about it at one point. She said c'mon down, fill out an application, see if you like it. Eight years later, I guess I liked it. [Laughs] I always thought that firefighters rode on the tailboard with the long coats and tall boots, but firefighting's definitely not what they put in the movies.

It was new for me, being eighteen and never having taken real orders from somebody. Then coming into an organization where there's a rank, there's a system. There's a chief, an assistant chief, battalion chiefs, lieutenants, sergeants, and the front-line guys. There was a lot of getting used to taking orders from people, people who were around my age. They're like "Go do this," and it was like "[grimaces]—I'm eighteen man—I don't want to listen to you." But you have to, and that was one of the hardest parts. But it's definitely helped me mature. I'm twenty-six now. I tend to listen more to people when they talk; I'm more open-minded when people talk. Then I see the millennials—even though that's my generation, but I see them and I'm like, "You should really respect people who are even a year, two years older than you. They've got that much more experience, that much more wisdom." I feel like my experience here has helped with that a lot.

Right now I'm doing 8 to 4, Monday through Friday, which isn't your typical fire department shift. It's usually a lot of 12s, or a 24 to 48 schedule [24 hours on, 48 hours off], or a 48 to 72 shift. Mine's more like an administrative, hourly shift. It's not bad; it's different. I went from working 24 to 48s when I did private ambulance, so I'd gotten used to that. I dropped that, came here, and was doing three or four 12s per week, depending on the week, with roughly a day off in between. You get used to doing that, but within a day it's like, you're not doing that, you're doing 8 to 4. I could go back to that—I love doing 24s.

Do you all sleep at the firehouse?
We have a bunk room upstairs, on the other side of my office. There are two beds in it, an air conditioner, a TV. It hooks directly into our overhead radio system so they can wake up. We provide sheets, towels, pillowcases.

Do you think there is a particular kind of person that's drawn to firefighting?
Everyone comes at it from different aspects of life. We have people who are pretty timid and learn to open up a little more. We have people who are excited 24/7 who learn to calm down a little bit, and some don't learn to calm down. Fire service in general attracts anybody and everybody. There's no one single person that wouldn't fit in. We have people of different ages. I'm twenty-six, and my paramedic today is forty-one. We have guys who are starting out who are seventeen, eighteen. We have guys who are starting out who are not even through the fire class yet and they're in their late thirties, early forties. I've seen people who never thought they could pick up a full-grown man and they've dragged him

fifty feet. The fire service opens up the box inside and lets out what that person can truly do.

We do physical fitness testing every year. One requirement is you have to be able to lift one of our 180-pound dummy mannequins and drag it fifty feet and then back fifty feet. There's a whole system we do for physical fitness—climb so many stairs in so many minutes, drag a rubber hose so many feet in such little time. Pick up tools and run them down the hallway and bring them back.

Do you feel like people inherently respect firefighters or appreciate what you do?

I think some people do like us and some don't, because they don't really know what we do and kind of see us like another form of the cops, that kind of thing. Sometimes people won't talk to us because they don't want to get in trouble, but the more we know, the better off you are so we can fix whatever's happening. Unless I'm on shift, I don't wear my uniform out in public because I don't want people to call me over and ask if they can do this or that [potentially dangerous thing related to fire in their backyard]. I think there is some admiration, but some people make fun of us, like we think we're so cool.

Are there any calls you particularly look forward to or really dread?

I always dread certain calls. The calls with children, that's a rough one. A structure fire with an entrapment, that's a rough one. I always keep that in the back of my mind—that can happen, that may happen. I always get an adrenaline rush depending on the call. EMS calls, you just get in the truck and go. That's kind of second nature at this point; you just get used to it. Anytime I get in the engine to go, I'm always a little pumped up, I'm hyped to go.

Has there been one call that has really stuck with you or made you realize you are doing exactly what you should be doing?

I can't pinpoint one call that's been career changing or life changing. You just kind of go out and help a complete stranger. Sometimes it's someone you know, and you help them in their worst moments, and you help get them out of that hole. Sometimes people are really sick, physically or mentally, and you've interjected this complete stranger in their life in that exact moment to help them. Sometimes you get out of it that it's a life-changing moment, or sometimes you're like, "Shit." It's not one call, it's all calls.

Do you think you'd ever want to work in a big city fire department?
Yes and no. I started here when I was eighteen. I grew up in this department, more or less. I was given a position of authority and trust. You get kind of used to working in this village department and it's a handful of guys and you all know each other. Then you get to a big city department and its 130 people. Would I love to work there? Yeah, I'm not going to lie. I'd like to work in a career department in Ohio, Boston, New York, LA. If given the chance, I'd really have to sit down and think about it. I'd be going from here [hand high up] to here [low hand] in a matter of days. It would be kinda different.

Would the work be much different, or is it the environment?
It's the environment that would be different. It's the same stuff we do here day to day—I've got a sheet of chores we're going to do today. "I'm going to do this, you're going to do that." Like scrubbing a toilet, cleaning the shower, doing the dishes, cleaning the coffeepot today, take the trash out, shred paper. And then we'll go check a truck, make sure it's ready to go. It's the same things any fire department across the country does every day. Make dinner, make lunch. [Either way], unless something crazy were to happen in the next couple of days or next couple of hours, I plan on doing this for a career. I plan on doing this for most of my life.

Old News from Miami Township and Selections from the *Yellow Springs News* Police Blotter, August 2015–December 2016

> There is no known society without entrenched criminality of
> different forms. No person exists whose morality is not daily
> infringed upon. Thus we must call crime necessary and declare
> that it cannot be non-existent, and that the very nature of
> social organization, as it is understood, logically implies it.
>
> —Émile Durkheim

Many readers of the *Yellow Springs News* note that the police blotter is the first thing they turn to with each week's paper, perhaps a holdover from the olden days when gossip was the preeminent form of entertainment. The interest in delving into the police report isn't surprising, as at least a few entries per week are a little unusual.

Every Monday, the writer responsible for writing the police report in the *Yellow Springs News* goes to the police station and picks up a manila folder with a printout of the preceding week's 911 call log. These entries are rewritten for the police report. Generally the items are self-explanatory and take only a line or two to report; other times the events are complex enough that a copy of the official documentation associated with the incident is requested for accuracy's sake. The writer of the police report is tacitly allowed to approach the assignment with a certain lightness of tone, reporting not with mockery but with a good-natured incredulity on the perplexing situations humans get themselves into. Who wouldn't laugh a little at the report of an adult with a bag over his head being pushed in a cart by a juvenile, or with the caller whose suspicious mail turned out to be nothing more than marketing offers?

But then again, anytime someone calls the police, they are in a situation where they feel desperate enough to call for help—in other words, at times when they are feeling particularly scared, unwell, angry, or confused. The police-blotter writer has to strike a delicate balance between recognizing an event's objective entertainment value while respecting the humanity of the people who happened to have ended up in the 911 call log. While most items are fairly harmless, the writer is quickly taken out of his reverie when a series of lighthearted calls gives way to a report of an attempted suicide or scene of domestic violence. The police report is not all fun and games and instead functions as a reminder of the tragic reality that many people experience as part of their daily life.

Appearing in the police blotter is not something people tend to have at the forefront of their minds when they call the police (though, technically, the 911 log is public record, so anything that appears in it is fair game for the paper). Many people have called the *News* and politely or forcefully requested that the item be pulled or details obscured so that nobody recognizes the offender. (The police blotter used to feature the full names of people charged with crimes, but this practice was stopped a decade ago, except in the cases of DUIs and minor traffic citations in an effort to make sure people are considered innocent until proven guilty.) While a request to pull an item usually isn't granted, the *News* would likely not run an item that would potentially result in real harm to the caller, and in most cases the report is vague enough that few people aside from the caller or perpetrator would know who was actually involved in the call.

But more often than not, the entries are enjoyed without too much guilt, snapshots of the relatively harmless foibles of small-town Ohio, a widely-agreed-upon source of entertainment in which you know that someday you may have a starring role. Even the people who called the police have to chuckle a little—sometimes all it takes is a little distance to see the lighter side of a situation.

A selection of some of the more noteworthy police blotter items from 2015 to 2016 is included below, following this item from *Xenia Daily Gazette* concerning the domestic adventures of a couple from Clifton. The article was published on July 10, 1885, and exemplifies the approach to reporting on semi-unbelievable events described above, reading like an expanded item from the police report. While a set of circumstances that is certainly reflective of repressive gender and marital roles, the wife in this scenario got the best of the situation with her pragmatic solution—find someone who will buy you the necessities you need when your spendthrift husband will not:

"Why she eloped—a Clifton woman leaves her home because her husband did not provide a new pair of shoes"

The village of South Charleston was thrown into an excitement Friday afternoon last by man running in to Squire Bradford's store just out of breath, exclaiming: "I want a warrant for a man what's run off with my wife." The Squire sent one of his boys with the man and told him to show this man Constable Way, and if he found the runaway he could then procure a warrant. The constable was soon found and they took themselves to the north end of the town, where the truant wife was lunching with her newly found Lord, a married man from Clifton, this county. Crackers and bologna devoured, Constable Way marched the whole crew to the City Hall, where it was found that the woman, Olie Brierly, was an old South Charleston lady, Olie Schindledecker, who, when less than 15 years of age married Lou Brierly, of Clifton. It appears that Olie was without shoes and, being a dutiful wife, asked Mr. Brierly to buy her a pair of shoes. But it being warm, he thought she could do for a while with the pair Nature gave her. There happened to be near by one, James Tilman, who had been winning the fair Olie's affections, and now she concluded she would strike for higher wages. Tilman and Olie struck out sometime Thursday, lying in the woods that night and arriving at South Charleston about three o' clock p.m. Friday, Olie still barefooted. Brierly obtained the service of one Lou Dudley, a colored man with a lot of blood hounds. Dudley started his dogs. The dogs came up with them as stated about three o'clock p.m., Friday.

Constable Way locked up "Tilman" and the fair Olie finally concluded she would return with her husband on a compromise that she was to have a new pair of shoes. After they had got out of town the constable let the other man out. He made tracks for Clifton lively. But such is life.

Verbatim Selections from the Police Report of the Yellow Springs News, August 2015–December 2016

On Aug. 10 police were dispatched to Peaches because a bearded, one-shoed man refused to leave the front patio. He eventually left in his vehicle but was pulled over a minute later for a busted taillight. The suspect was given a sobriety test and taken to the police department, where he removed a clock from the wall in the interview room.

On Wednesday, Aug. 12 a caller reported that a "pink Razor scooter with cool flashing LED lights in the wheels and a flaming kick tail was heartlessly stolen" from outside the Montessori school on the Antioch campus.

On Aug. 14 a caller reported that she is the subject of repeated calls from a collection agency even though she is not the target of their collections. She has asked them repeatedly not to call her but the calls continue. The officer called the collection agency and explained the situation, and the agency said they won't call her anymore.

On Wednesday, Aug. 19 police responded to a call about a "white van full of squatters" on N. College that had been there for a couple of days. The squatters were deemed legitimate—they are working with the student union.

A classic rivalry played out on Park Place on Aug. 23: the postmaster reported that a mail carrier was bitten by a dog. Greene County Animal Control and a medic were dispatched to the scene.

On Aug. 23 a caller advised that someone took her cell phone and threw it in the trash.

On Aug. 23 a dead skunk was reported on Meadow Lane. The dispatcher advised that if the skunk is on public property Animal Control will pick it up. It was determined that the skunk was on private property and so the homeowner was responsible for it.

Police followed up the skunk situation a little while later on Aug. 23. Police said they would help remove the skunk if the owner had a trash bag. The officer removed the skunk from the property and disposed of it.

On Aug. 25 a caller reported the theft of medicine and a bag of chips from the counter of the BP on Xenia Avenue.

On Aug. 30 a caller reported an adult with a bag over his head being pushed in a cart by a juvenile in the area of W. North College Street and Xenia.

On Aug. 30 a caller reported a Pepsi machine on fire outside of Tom's Market. The fire was extinguished.

On Wednesday, Sept. 2 a caller complained that his neighbor's chickens continually invade his yard in the 300-block of Dayton Street. The owner of the chickens said that she has fencing material and will build a fence soon.

On Sept. 3 a caller reported that she was worried her dog killed a neighbor's chicken on Northwood Drive, but the chicken's caretaker determined that the chicken was fine.

On Sept. 3 police were advised that a customer at Yellow Springs Brewery was intoxicated and wasn't acting quite right, even for an intoxicated person. The subject fell over and hit his face on the pavement while speaking with police and was remanded to the custody of his mother.

At 1:46 a.m. on Friday, Sept. 4 a caller on King Street reported that someone threw an egg at his front door. The responding officer checked neighboring homes for evidence of other eggs thrown and found egg remnants on the sidewalk a few houses down.

Chickens continued to invade a neighbor's yard on Sept. 5. The responding officer rounded up six chickens and four ducks. The fowl owner said she would put up a fence that day.

On Monday, September 14 a teacher was transported from the Greene County Educational Service Center to the hospital after being bitten by a sixth-grader.

At 3:29 a.m. on Sept. 18 Antioch security told police that no less than two bricks were thrown through a window of a building on campus in under an hour.

On Sept. 18 police assisted a family whose daughter had jumped out the car on the way to meet her probation officer.

On Sept. 18 a caller wanted to report an "unruly juvenile, not hers."

On Sept. 28 screams echoing through the neighborhood drew police officers to a home on the 500 block of Union Court. It was determined that the screams were coming from the homeowner's son and his friends playing video games in the garage. They were asked to keep it down.

On Sept. 29 a driver suspected of driving under the influence was found to be "just very upset." He was followed home by officers.

On Oct. 14 an Antioch Library librarian called regarding library books checked out from the library in a car that was repossessed after the owner died. Police informed the librarian that the possessions in the car were disposed of.

A caller on Dayton Street told police he was worried about "four guys with flashlights checking the breaker box" on Dayton Street at 8:47 a.m. on Oct. 19 because he thought it was too early in the morning for that kind of work to be done. Police confirmed that it was a legitimate construction crew working with the breakers.

On Oct. 20 a father turned his daughter's gun in to the police. The daughter came in to the station to pick it up a few hours later.

On Oct. 21 a caller reported that a male and two friends were rude when questioned why they parked near a dumpster at the BP.

On Oct. 23 police explained the Village Mediation Program to a homeowner on Limestone Street who has a problem with her neighbor's landscaping light. The light is 50 watts and deep in the neighbor's property, meaning that the offended neighbor doesn't have any legal ground to complain.

Police received a call at 10:48 a.m. on Nov. 3 wondering why some "teenagers" were at the Glass Farm and not in school. Police found that it was a 5th grade class studying the habitat of area animals.

On Nov. 3 a caller reported that several people started yelling at the priest during a parish meeting at St. Paul's Catholic Church.

A caller reported that a dog had its head stuck in a fence between two properties on Omar Circle on Nov. 5. The officer helped free the poor beast.

A caller reported seeing a bike in the bushes near a house on W. Center College Street on Nov. 10. The officer noted that he too has seen many bikes in the area of the same bushes.

On Thursday, Nov. 12 a caller reported that she found "an overnight travel bag on her front porch and thought it was her boyfriend's, but when she opened it [she found] it was full of hypodermic needles." The bag was determined to belong to a neighbor and was medically appropriate.

On Saturday, Nov. 14 a caller reported that when he was walking his dog a woman in a red coat told him that if he shined a flashlight at her again she would cut him. In turn, he said he would shoot her because he has a concealed-carry permit. An officer told the man to put the gun away and then came to speak with him.

On Nov. 15 three drunken carousers hopped in the truck belonging to the food vendor in the BP parking lot. Someone saw the taillights go on in the truck and investigated, which prompted the men to scatter throughout downtown. Police were on the lookout for the suspects at various locales. The three were eventually found and one was cited for disorderly conduct.

A resident on Greene Street reported on Nov. 17 that the three children living in a house near him scream "bloody murder all hours of the day and night," to the degree that "all neighbors are desensitized by the constant screaming."

At 2:47 a.m. on Sunday, Nov. 22 a caller reported that her juvenile son had gotten in her face after she asked him to pick up the mess he had made on the floor. The caller said she just wanted officers to talk to her son about the disrespect he is showing her. An officer spoke with her son and the son apologized to his mother.

A caller reported a hit-skip on Meadow Lane involving a vehicle pulling a stump-grinder on Dec. 3.

On Dec. 12 a caller reported that the steel drummer had been playing in the same spot for three hours. Police made contact with the drummer and he said he would move down the street. Police received another complaint about the steel drummer playing in one place for too long on Dec. 12. He again said he would move.

On Dec. 13 a caller requested an officer take a look at suspicious mail he had received. The officer checked the website listed on the mail and determined it was a marketing offer.

On Dec. 17 police received a dispatch that a truck was selling meat door-to-door on Northwood Drive. An officer told the driver that a permit is needed to sell articles in this way, and of this type.

On Jan. 3 a caller reported that she received a visit from a woman who had given her a dog last spring. She wanted to see the dog, but because they had had a falling out, the caller refused. The visitor threatened to report the dog as stolen. Police checked and found the dog was registered with

Animal Control. The officer reported the dog appeared to be in good health and lived with the caller; the complaint was deemed a civil matter.

On Friday, Jan. 8 at approximately 9 p.m. a caller reported he had seen three males come out of a manhole near the Yellow Springs sculpture with lights on their heads.

On Jan. 26 a father requested an officer speak with his son about not being disrespectful in the home. The son made a verbal agreement to be more cooperative.

A caller reported that the sax player had been playing in the same location for over three hours on Jan. 30.

On Feb. 23 police were advised that three boys were throwing rocks at "construction stuff" and had run off when the caller yelled at them. Police were on the lookout for the little scamps.

On Feb. 27 police were alerted to two subjects who may have taken some cheese from Tom's Market. The two were located at the laundromat, where one subject admitted to urinating behind a dumpster because of a new urination-increasing medication. He said he'd try to conceal himself, and police advised him not to cause alarm to others.

An ID from the Czech Republic was found on Corry Street on Feb. 29.

A caller reported on Mar. 7 that a dead squirrel was hung in a tree outside his house. He felt foul play might be involved because someone had removed a few dead limbs from the same tree last year. Police and the subject agreed that it was possible the squirrel had fallen and gotten caught, and the homeowner said he'd remove the squirrel.

On Mar. 31 a juvenile male threatened to beat up another juvenile male in the Bryan Center. The dispute was referred to the authority of the Recreation Room monitors.

On Apr. 9 officers were dispatched to Gaunt Park in reference to someone seeing a machete stuck in the ground. Officers postulated that the machete was left behind by workers doing surveying work. The machete was placed into the evidence room.

Screams reported coming from the Glen on Apr. 25 were determined to be from wildlife.

On Tuesday, Apr. 26 at 1:45 a.m. police determined that the passengers of cars parked in the Speedway parking lot were just switching vehicles.

On Apr. 26 a caller on President Street reported a "shovel-load of horse manure maliciously dumped on his property."

A caller reported finding a purse with cancelled checks and other personal items in it on Apr. 30. Police made contact with the owner who said she deliberately threw it away.

On May 5 officers returned a completed and signed golf cart inspection form to some homeowners.

On Sunday, May 8 dispatch received a call about a sick raccoon on Xenia Avenue. Police were on scene with the raccoon, who put it in a box and released it into the Glen.

On Tuesday, May 17 police dispatched a medic to help a teenager with "painful eyes."

Police informed a driver on May 19 that her handicap placard was no longer valid because the person to who[m] it was registered was no longer living. The driver said she thought the placard was registered in her mother's name and would get it changed.

On May 21 dispatch received a call that a man with a preexisting head injury was upset over losing his hat.

A caller reported on May 23 that a deer fell into the open basement of a house that was being built. Animal control and police were able to remove the deer.

A teenager called police on May 24 to report that "all his mother would do was yell and scream at him," and he didn't know why. The argument was over when police arrived.

On May 30 police realized there is no ordinance on shooting air soft guns inside the village upon responding to an incident on West Limestone.

A caller reported someone had put some stickers with questionable and possibly offensive meaning on an electrical box on E. Enon Road and Dayton Street on June 7. Police photographed the stickers and removed them.

Street Fair incident roundup: on June 11, the following happened at street fair—a phone charger was found, a six-year-old got separated from her parents, police jumped a truck for a vendor, a phone was found run over in a parking lot, and

police made contact with a subject in a kilt, who prom-
ised there would be no more dancing around.

Police gave chase on June 12 through the Glen Forest cemetery, past
the Brewery, and then down Walnut after two subjects
who took off running after flagging down an officer.

On June 21 a caller reported that a vehicle had been at a gas pump for
45 minutes, and that the owner had just staggered around
the corner.

A caller on West Whiteman reported loud voices on the block behind
his home on June 23. An officer encountered juveniles
playing with capes and machetes. The juveniles were
"told to have fun but to remember that neighbors have
windows open and can hear what is being said."

A caller reported on June 30 that someone had spray painted her
trash can, the street, and a nearby telephone switch box.
A neighbor advised the culprit was her son.

On Sunday, July 10, a juvenile was banned from the Glen until he is
18 for repeatedly carving he [sic] and his girlfriend's ini-
tials into the trees.

At 3:07 a.m. on Saturday, July 23, a caller flagged down an officer
after seeing juveniles throwing eggs on South High Street.
The officer found an egg carton on the street filled with
crushed eggs, but the juveniles were gone upon arrival.

Police received an alert that there were dogs inside a hot car in front
of Haha Pizza on July 24. When they arrived, they found
the dog's caretakers were just picking up pizza, and the
windows of the vehicle were down and the dogs had
plenty of water.

On Saturday, July 30 a resident came into the police station to
speak with an officer about a product he bought online
at Kmart. The item was purchased in his wife's name
and sent to the store. Although he had her ID, the store
wouldn't accept it or allow him to pick it up. He reported
that he took the item anyway.

A caller reported on Aug. 3, that a "little fellow" was running around
the area of North Winter Street. When the caller he asked
the kid if he was alright [sic], the kid said "leave me
alone."

At 1:07 a.m. on Sunday, Aug. 7 police spotted several teenagers running down Wright Street toward Gaunt Park. The teenag-

ers were heading to the pool. Two escaped while police caught one and turned him over to his mother.

On Tuesday, Aug. 9 a caller reported that five intoxicated subjects were riding bikes toward downtown, and were pulling suitcases behind them.

On Tuesday, Sept. 6, police spoke with a resident of Omar Circle regarding making other living arrangements for his rooster. He was given a few days to accomplish the task.

Police were alerted of an underage smoker on state route 370 and an adult subject stabbing the ground with a knife. However, police found that the knife was a camping knife and the people were in fact camping. The subjects said they are going to put the knife away.

On Tuesday, September 27, at 4:19 a.m., a caller reported that a man wearing a thermal mask came out into the roadway toward her vehicle. The caller did not stop. Police located the man and found that he was attempting to get a light for his cigarette.

On Sept. 27 a caller reported three young males swordfighting with fake swords and requested that police make contact with them. Police found that the men were trying out home-made wooden swords.

On Friday, Sept. 30, a caller requested a check of the area when her daughter reported someone banging on the door and saying that the clowns are here.

On Wednesday, Oct. 12, an officer found a wallet behind Nipper's Corner, but found that it was too weathered to make an accurate inventory of its contents.

On Oct. 12 a resident came into the police station for assistance with getting her cast readjusted, as it melted slightly when she sat next to a space heater. An officer was able to cut off enough foam that it could be comfortably worn.

On Oct. 16, officers investigated subjects walking around Ellis Pond with flashlights, and found that they were "possibly looking for beavers."

On Oct. 17 a caller reported that someone had stolen all of the mums she had placed around her mailbox.

On Oct. 18 a caller reported that someone had been in her house while she was at work, as cabinets were open and hamburger was left out on the counter.

On Oct. 22 a caller reported two individuals verbally fighting outside of the hotel. It turned out that the bride was very intoxicated and had to be taken to the hospital, and the brother of the bride and another sister were arguing about it. The police reported "there was no other problem than a highly intoxicated bride."

On Oct. 24 a caller reported that a cat had been hit by a car and killed on Union Street. Neighbors did not recognize the cat, and it was laid to rest on Sutton Farm. However, the cat's caretaker came into the police station and was upset the cat had already been buried. An officer went to the farm to exhume the cat and return it to the owner. It turned out that it was not the right cat, and the officer returned to the farm to rebury it.

A young boy was tested for alcohol ingestion on Nov. 11 after he reported to his mother that an icee his dad bought him "tasted funny." The test showed no evidence of alcohol consumption.

Police received a call on Saturday, Nov. 12 from a male who said that a female was throwing all of his property out of the house. During the call, the female grabbed the phone, stated everything was fine and hung up.

A caller reported losing her change purse, possibly at a garage sale, on Nov. 12. She then realized she likely lost it in a different town and said she'd file a report there. A few hours later, she spoke with police and claimed the purse was stolen by the resident who hosted the garage sale. Police attempted to contact the resident but couldn't make contact.

On Friday. Dec. 16, a caller requested that someone from the Village pick up a tire in an alley near Green Street. It was not determined where the tire came from.

SOURCES

Bakari vs. Mays et al. 2010 Ohio. Accessed January 2, 2017. https://dockets. justia.com/docket/ohio/ohsdc e/3:2010cv00250/139235.

Banta, R. E. *The Ohio*. Ohio River Valley Series. Louisville: University of Kentucky Press, 1949, 1998.

Broadstone, Michael A. *History of Greene County, Ohio: Its People, Industries and Institutions*. Indianapolis: B. F. Brown and Co., Inc., 1918.

Committee of the Home Coming Association, eds. "Miami Township." In *Greene County 1803–1908*. Xenia: Aldine Publishing, 1908.

"Digging Deeper . . . a Greene County B&B Story." Green County Combined Health District Annual Report 2015. Accessed December 19, 2016. http://www.gcph.info/files/announcements/attachments/376_Annual_ Report_2015.pdf.

Dills, R. S. *History of Greene County, Together with Historic Notes on the Northwest, and the State of Ohio*. Dayton: Odell and Mayer, 1881.

Downes, Randolph C. *Evolution of Ohio County Boundaries*. Columbus: The Ohio Historical Society, 1927 and 1970.

Fitrakis, Bob. "Did U.S. Intelligence Assets Kill Antioch College?" Accessed October 27, 2016. https://freepress.org/article/did-us-intelligence-assets-kill-antioch-college.

———. "Shock, Awe and Antioch: The Bush Administration's Attack on Progressive Education." Accessed October 27, 2016. https://freepress.org/ article/shock-awe-and-antioch-bush-administrations-attack-progressive-education.

Galloway, William Albert. *The History of Glen Helen.* Originally published 1932; reprinted in 1977 by The Bookmark, Knightstown, Indiana, and sponsored by the Glen Helen Association.

Gartman, Don. "A Natural for James Michener." *Columbia Today* (Spring 1984).

"Greene County, Ohio—A Study of the Structure and Functions of County Government." The League of Women Voters of Fairborn, Xenia, and Yellow Springs, 1970.

Howe, Henry. *Historical Collections of Ohio in Two Volumes.* Published by the State of Ohio, 1888.

Hutslar, Donald A. "The Driverless Coach." *Echoes* 1, no. 10 (October 1962).

McCullough, Stafford. "The Whiteman Settlement at Clifton." Self-published: 1937. Retrieved from the Xenia Library Greene County Room.

"Ohio Lands." Pamphlet published by the office of Jim Petro, Auditor of State, 1997.

Ohio Township Trustee Sourcebook. Miami: Center for Public Management and Regional Affairs, Miami University in conjunction with the Ohio Township Association, 2013.

Portrait and Biographical Album of Greene and Clark Counties, Ohio. Chicago: Chapman Brothers, 1890.

Robinson, George F. *History of Greene County, Ohio.* . . . Chicago: S. J. Clarke Publishing Company, 1902.

Southwest Ohio Branch APWA. "Snow and Ice Control Conference" 2015 pamphlet.

Talbert, Robert. "Antioch College and Vast Conspiracies Redux." Accessed October 10, 2016. http://www.chronicle.com/blognetwork/ castingoutnines/2007/08/25/antioch-college-and-vast-conspiracies-redux/.

———. "Tinfoil Hats versus Accounting." Accessed October 10, 2016. http://www.chronicle.com/blognetwork/castingoutnines/2007/07/17/ tinfoil-hats-versus-accounting/.

U.S. Census Department. "Populations of Interest—Municipalities and Townships. Accessed January 5, 2017. http://www.census.gov/govs/go/munici- pal_township_govs.html.

Warren Commission Hearings. Accessed May 5, 2016. http://www.history- matters.com/archive/jfk/ wc/wcvols/contents.htm.

Willson, Catherine Kidd. *Historic Greene County: An Illustrated History.* Commissioned by the Greene County Historical Society and published by the Historical Publishing Network, 2010.

Woodward, Susan L. and Jerry N. McDonald. *Indian Mounds of the Middle Ohio Valley.* Blacksburg, VA: The McDonald and Woodward Publishing Company, 2002.

These invaluable works of civic brilliance:

The Ohio Revised Code
The Yellow Springs Village Charter
The Miami Township Code

Extended personal interviews with:

Chris Mucher; Mark Crockett; Lamar Spracklen; Margaret Silliman; Zo Van Eaton-Meister; Richard Zopf; Dan Gochenouer; Erik and Deirdre Owen, and Luisa Owen; Bill and Jody Farrar; Deb Leopold, Director of Environmental Health Services at the Greene County Combined Health District; Nora Byrnes; Colin Altman; Nate Ayers.

Newspapers:

This book relies heavily on articles printed in many area newspapers, both extant and long since closed. The Greene County room at the Xenia branch of the Greene County Library System has a substantial collection of clippings neatly organized by township, as does the Greene County Historical Society. These archives were invaluable, as were contemporary articles from the *Xenia Gazette,* the *Fairborn Daily Herald,* the *Springfield News-Sun,* and the *Dayton Daily News.* This book certainly wouldn't have been possible without countless articles from the inimitable, award-winning *Yellow Springs News.*

DVDs:

Thanks to Susan Gartner of the Village of Yellow Springs for burning DVD copies of the videos of the September 9 and September 21 township trustee meetings.

ABOUT THE AUTHOR

Dylan Taylor-Lehman is a nonfiction writer from southeastern Ohio. Previously a reporter for the *Yellow Springs News,* he also writes about Bigfoot, micronations, and landfills. He graduated from The Ohio State University with a degree in English and then set out to try as many jobs as possible, which led to "memorable" stints as a professional mover, carpenter, and black mold eradicator. Now, he vastly prefers poring over dusty old histories and being holed up and writing for days on end. He currently lives in El Paso, Texas, and looks forward to checking out the minor civil jurisdictions in other states and countries.